Ex Libris

Gandy Manning

INTRODUCTION
TO THE THEORY OF
EMPLOYMENT

INTRODUCTION
TO THE THEORY OF
EMPLOYMENT

JOAN ROBINSON

SECOND EDITION

MACMILLAN
ST MARTIN'S PRESS

First Edition 1937
Reprinted 1938 (twice), 1939
Reissued 1947
Reprinted 1947, 1949, 1952, 1956, 1960, 1964
Second Edition 1969
Reprinted 1970, 1971

Published by
THE MACMILLAN PRESS LTD
London and Basingstoke
Associated companies in New York Toronto
Dublin Melbourne Johannesburg and Madras

SBN 333 04395 2

Printed in Great Britain by
REDWOOD PRESS LIMITED
Trowbridge and London

CONTENTS

CHAPTER V

CHAPTER VI

CHAPTER VII

CHAPTER VIII

CHAPTER IX

CONTENTS

CHAPTER X

CHANGES IN THE SUPPLY OF MONEY

CHAPTER XI

FOREIGN TRADE

CHAPTER XII

CHANGES IN EMPLOYMENT

CHAPTER XIII

CONTROVERSY IN ECONOMICS

PREFACE TO THE SECOND EDITION

AFTER THIRTY YEARS

THIS little book has some interest as an historical document. It belongs to the period when Keynes was battering at the walls of orthodoxy to gain an entry for the view that it was possible, and necessary, for governments to take measures to reduce unemployment.

The doctrines of Marshall and Pigou, whom Keynes attacked in the *General Theory*, were never very coherently stated; nowadays we can see what was the concealed basis of their logic, and some of their implicit concepts have been brought into the open and clearly expressed in modern terms. There were two branches to the orthodox theory, one for the stationary state and one for a process of accumulation.

In the stationary state, there was a quantity of "capital" made of a substance like putty which could be squeezed into various forms in no time and without cost. The wage bargain was made in real terms. Unemployment could be due only to the wage being fixed too high; if workers would only accept a lower wage it would become profitable to offer more employment — the putty would be squeezed out so as to make use of less "capital intensive" methods of production.

In a growing economy, there was a certain amount of saving that the population desired to make out of the incomes that they would enjoy when full employment obtained. Unemployment could arise only from a failure of entrepreneurs to use all the savings for investment, that is to say, from the rate of interest being too high. If the savers would only offer funds at a lower rate, investment would equal saving and full employment would be ensured.

Such doctrines, of course, were never clearly set out. They were implied by authoritative statements, such as Professor Gregory's Addendum to the Macmillan Report,[1] which advocated a cut in money-wage rates as the best remedy for a slump, or the Treasury view, that there is a certain amount of saving available in any period so that if the Government borrows more of it to carry out investment at home there will be an exactly offsetting fall in investment overseas.[2] These were the fallacies which this introduction to Keynes' *General Theory* was trying to expose.

The war proved Keynes' point and a new orthodoxy came into the ascendant. The White Paper of 1944 on Employment Policy,[3] opens with the words :

> The Government accept as one of their primary aims and responsibilities the maintenance of a high and stable level of employment.

This is a much more complicated undertaking than to reduce unemployment from a high level. In a deep slump, when orthodoxy maintained that nothing could be done, it was necessary only to argue in favour of expenditure of any kind — to pay men to dig holes in the ground would be better than doing nothing. A policy to maintain near-full employment once it has been reached must be much more selective. In particular, it turns out to be far from simple to maintain a high level of effective demand at

[1] *Report of the Committee on Finance and Industry* (1931).
[2] See *Memoranda on Certain Proposals Relating to Unemployment*, Cmd. 3331 (1929).
[3] Cmd. 6527.

home together with an adequate balance of payments abroad.

Moreover, once the duty to maintain full employment is accepted, the whole moral and political basis of the argument changes. If we are to be guaranteed full employment in any case, the question to be discussed is what the employment should be for. Do we want more investment or more consumption? If more investment, should it be in the infra-structure of industry — the supply of power, transport and communications — should it be in private profit-seeking business or should it be in the improvement of social services — education, health, housing — and general amenities? If more consumption, should it be to reduce poverty or to give everyone a proportionate share?

These deep, divisive questions are smoothed over by making employment an end in itself. Since Keynes became orthodox, full employment has become a conservative slogan.

Keynes' theory of prices took much longer to be universally accepted. The main point which he had to make was that a cut in money-wage rates, far from helping to increase employment, would reduce prices, increase the burden of debt and discourage investment; but the converse proposition, that raising money wages would raise prices, was just as much part of his system, as Chapter VII bears witness.

Keynes was not much interested in the theory of imperfect competition, though he had given my book on that subject a vague blessing. He thought of the share of gross profit in the value of current sales as being governed by the difference between marginal and average costs. Nowadays we think in terms of administered prices, and of gross margins, in the main, as fixed by the policy of oligopolistic firms. In either case, an all-round rise of money-wage rates, which raises all prime costs (abstracting from foreign trade), brings a more or less proportional rise in the general price level. With perfect competition (if such a thing were conceivable) the adjustment would be automatic; with imperfect competition an element of policy enters in; sometimes the firms may find it politic to allow margins to be squeezed a little; sometimes they may take advantage of a rise in prime costs to raise prices more than proportionately.

Just as the war converted public opinion to the notion that governments must be concerned with employment, so years of creeping inflation have converted the authorities to the need for a " prices and incomes policy ", which, in crude terms, means the control of money-wage rates. This also has a conservative bias, though the trade unions could learn from Keynes how the system really works and what demands they could most effectively make.

The third main strand in Keynes' thought — the theory of the rate of interest — has not worn so well. Certainly the old tendency to confuse interest, which is the cost of borrowing, with profit, which is the return on investment, and the idea that the rate of interest is determined by demand and supply of real investible resources, were swept away; but the positive part of Keynes' analysis (which was followed in this little book) is now seen to attribute too much importance to the rate of interest as a regulator of the economy. This part of Keynes' teaching was a concession to earlier doctrines and to weaken it is to separate his system all the more decisively from the old orthodoxy.

Keynes was urgently concerned to bring analysis to bear upon the immediate problem of the breakdown of the market economy. He did not think much about long-period problems. When he did throw out some ideas on the subject, he suggested that, with peace and the cessation of the growth of population, a country such as ours, by maintaining investment at the full-employment rate, could complete all the accumulation that would be useful to society within a generation. (Since neither precondition has been fulfilled we cannot calculate how far out he was.)

The fashion has now changed; economic theory is concerned with perpetual growth. This raises a fresh set of questions, but they can by no means dispense with Keynes. A pre-Keynesian theory, in which capital is made of putty and the rate of interest is determined by the supply of saving, is no more use for these problems than it was for the problem of employment. What is now needed is a generalisation of the General Theory, to carry it into fields which Keynes had no time to enter.

* * *

The reader may find it convenient to look at the following notes after reading the relevant parts of the text.

There are a number of points in the formal structure of the *General Theory* which have caused trouble. One of these is the treatment of the proposition that savings are equal to investment both as an accounting identity and as a causal relationship (Chapters II and III).

As an identity, it means that when we set out the statistics of national income for, say, a year by double entry, showing the sources of income and its expenditure (with a balanced budget and no foreign trade), outlay on gross investment is necessarily shown as equal to the excess of income over outlay on consumption — that is, to saving *plus* amortisation allowances. This played an important part in the controversy around the *General Theory*, for it served to eliminate some prevalent fancies, such as that saving exceeds investment by the amount of " hoarding " (see page 12).

As a causal relationship, the proposition expresses a view of how a modern economy works. Decisions to invest influence the level of income and the rate of saving, while decisions to save do not directly influence the level of investment.

Keynes postulated that, in a given short-period situation, there is a stable, predictable relationship between the level of household incomes and the amount of expenditure on consumption appropriate to it. If this were the case, and if the time-lags involved were short, it would be correct to say that the rate of savings at every moment is equated to the rate of investment by the level of income. This assumption underlies the exposition of the Multiplier. The Multiplier represents the change in income appropriate to a change in investment. When time-lags are not negligible, the income appropriate to one level of investment cannot, in general, be reached before the level of investment has changed, so that exact equality between the rate of investment and the *appropriate* rate of saving would never be established. At each moment some of the saving would be inappropriate — rather too high immediately after an unexpected rise of income or too low after a recent fall.

A great fuss was made over this point by some critics who were not trying to improve Keynes' exposition but to attack his basic ideas.

A more substantial problem is now being experienced. At the level of income that we have been enjoying recently, the propensity to consume is by no means as reliable as

Keynes supposed. This is one of the major difficulties that beset policies intended to control employment and prices with the limited means available to a modern government.

A serious weakness in the formal scheme of the *General Theory* is the proposition that the rate of investment tends to be such as to equate the prospective rate of profit (" the marginal efficiency of capital ") to the rate of interest. To say that the expected return on investment *allowing for risk* is equal to the rate of interest (see page 23) is nothing but a fudge ; the allowance for risk, as Keynes emphasised in other parts of his book, will be high or low according to the state of confidence. A calculation of the profits required to justify a scheme of investment always shows a large excess over the market rate of interest. Since both expected profits and apprehensions of risk are partly subjective views in the minds of entrepreneurs, there is no way of separating them out. If the excess of profits over interest is defined as the allowance for risk, then expected profits allowing for risk are equal to the rate of interest merely by definition ; the proposition tells us nothing. It was a sound instinct that made me choose house-building as an example of a scheme of investment (page 24), for in that case the influence of the rate of interest is much more definite and calculable.

The allusion to armaments as a booster to employment (page 27) has gained a grim relevance in modern times.

Another weakness in Keynes' formal scheme is the failure to allow for the effect of investment itself, through current receipts, upon prospective profits. Importing some ideas from Michal Kalecki, I improved somewhat upon Keynes' treatment of the trade cycle (Chapter XII). However, there are some points in this argument which I would not want to defend today. One is the idea that recovery from a deep slump could come about automatically without a fresh boost from outside (see pages 91–2). Another is the notion (page 94) that a boom tends to check itself by driving up the rate of interest and making borrowing too expensive. This was part of the usual exposition of Keynes' theory, but it is obviously absurd, for it cannot be true that it is harder to borrow in a boom than in a slump.

The adumbration of stop-go policy on page 96 has turned out to be prescient, but the reference to the prospects of population growth and a new age of inventions on page 98 is notably wide of the mark.

The treatment of money and the rate of interest (Chapters VIII to X) is extremely primitive, but it may be useful as a warning against some pre-Keynesian ideas that are nowadays being revived.

The treatment of the relation between inequality and thriftiness (Chapter V) has gained a great deal of point in recent times.

JOAN ROBINSON

January 1969

FOREWORD

THE purpose of this book is to provide a simplified account of the main principles of the Theory of Employment for students who find that they require some help in assimilating Mr. Keynes' *General Theory of Employment, Interest and Money*, and the literature which is growing round it. In writing a book of this kind there is necessarily a conflict between the claims of rigour and of simplicity. In the present case it is rigour that has been sacrificed where need be, and the reader must regard this book merely as a preparation for deeper studies. Besides the *General Theory*, I have drawn upon my own *Essays in the Theory of Employment*, Mr. Colin Clark's *National Income and Outlay* and Mr. Michal Kalecki's article, " A Theory of the Business Cycle ", in the *Review of Economic Studies*, February 1937. I have done my best to resist the temptation to address my colleagues over the heads of the audience for which this book is properly intended, and it is not designed to help in the resolution of the controversies which are at present disturbing the world of academic economics.

JOAN ROBINSON

CAMBRIDGE
August 1937

CHAPTER I

INTRODUCTION

INTRODUCTORY

THE modern economic system fails to provide employment continuously for all who desire to work. This is generally recognised as one of the major defects of the system, and remedies for the defect are constantly being propounded. Diagnosis must precede prescription, and the following pages attempt to do no more than to assist the reader to the first elementary stages of an understanding of the disease.

The reader may be inclined to ask, " If it is possible to understand what causes trade prosperity, why do we not immediately set about to secure it ? " That, indeed, is a hard question. Economic life presents us always with a choice of evils and no course of policy is the best for everyone. There will always be some who prefer the disease to any possible treatment that can be proposed for it, and the question of remedies remains in dispute even when the diagnosis is agreed upon. This volume is intended to guide the reader towards an understanding of the problem, but not to tell him what ought to be done.

DEFICIENCY OF DEMAND

Under a system of private enterprise it is, in a simple and obvious sense, the decisions of employers — in the main, industrial entrepreneurs — which determine the amount of employment offered to the working population, but the entrepreneurs themselves are subject to general influences which cause them to decide one way or another, and the decisions of each influence the decisions of the rest. There is no central control, no plan of action, and whatever actually occurs in economic life is the result of innumerable independent individual decisions. The course which it is best for each individual to pursue in his own interests is rarely the same as the course best calculated to promote the interests of society as a whole, and if our economic system appears sometimes fantastic or even insane — as when foodstuffs are destroyed while men go hungry — we must remember that it is not surprising that the interaction of free individual decisions should lead so often to irrational, clumsy and bewildering results.

Under this system, goods and services are produced in order that they may be sold profitably. Thus the output of goods and services that will be produced depends upon the demand for them. "Demand" implies money expenditure, not desire or need. No matter how great a man's need may be for goods to feed and clothe and amuse him, he cannot make it worth anyone's while to produce them for him unless he has money to pay, and need does not constitute "demand" unless it is accompanied by expenditure. As we know only too well, in the economic system under which we live, it often happens that productive resources are unemployed — men out of work, machines idle, land falling out of cultivation — while at the same time there is bitter need for the goods which they are able to produce. Output falls below its possible maximum, not when needs are satiated, but when demand is deficient.

How can a deficiency of demand come about? The demand for goods on the part of individual consumers is governed mainly by their income. The larger the income *not necessarily*

an individual has the greater will be his expenditure on current consumption. But income is the product of expenditure as well as the source of expenditure. Men earn their incomes by supplying each other's demands. One man's expenditure provides other men's incomes, and one man's income is derived from other men's expenditure. From this we might be inclined to argue that if resources are idle at any moment it must be the result merely of an accident or mismanagement, for all that is necessary is to increase activity, and incomes will increase so as to provide a demand for the extra goods produced.

But the whole of everyone's income is not spent on current consumption. Provided the standard of life of an individual is above a certain bare minimum, he may want to save part of his income in order to build up a store of wealth. Wealth is accumulated in order to provide security against future emergencies, to satisfy the lust of possession, or to acquire further income by lending it at interest. For motives of this kind, individuals put aside part of their income, and acquire wealth, by means of consuming less than the full amount of goods which their income could purchase. This would cause no trouble if the decision to save led directly to a demand for real capital — houses, machines, ships and so forth. For in that case the part of income saved would give employment in making capital goods just as the part spent on consumption gives employment in making consumption goods. The desire to save could not then be a cause of unemployment.

But the demand for capital goods comes, not from saving, but from business concerns who use them in production, and no entrepreneur is inclined to acquire capital goods unless he can see a profit by doing so. The

3

mere fact that individuals want to save part of their incomes to add to their private wealth does nothing to encourage entrepreneurs to expect a greater profit from capital. The profitability of capital goods depends upon the demand for the consumption goods which they produce. Thus if individuals decide to save, that is, not to spend on immediate consumption, they reduce rather than increase the motive of the entrepreneurs for acquiring new capital goods, and the decision to save reduces the demand for consumption goods without increasing the demand for capital goods.

It is for this reason that unemployment can occur. There is unemployment when the decisions of entrepreneurs as to how much new capital it is worth their while to acquire fall short of the desire of individuals to save. Saving depletes the demand for consumption goods, for saving means not spending upon current consumption, and the entrepreneurs fail to make up for it by creating a sufficient demand for capital goods to fill the gap. Then demand is deficient and men and machines stand idle, not because humanity has no *need* for their services, but because *demand* is not great enough for anyone to be able to make a profit for himself by setting them to work.

SYNOPSIS

The next four chapters will be devoted to following out the clue which we have here picked up — that the level of demand, and consequently of employment, depends upon the interaction between the desire to save and the desire to invest in real capital. Chapter II (Investment and Saving) outlines this system of ideas. Chapter III (The Multiplier) describes in more detail the effect of a change in investment upon employment and

Chapter IV discusses the reasons for which a change in investment may occur. Chapter V (Changes in Thriftiness) is devoted to the desire to save. We are now possessed of the major part of the theory of employment, but there are some more pieces of the jig-saw puzzle which must be collected before we can make a complete picture. Prices and the monetary system have still to be considered. After glancing at some miscellaneous points in Chapter VI, we turn to the subject of the price level in Chapter VII. Chapter VIII introduces the important topic of the rate of interest, and shows in what way the workings of the monetary system are connected with the influences which determine employment. The next two chapters (Aspects of the Rate of Interest and Changes in the Supply of Money) are each, in a certain sense, a digression from our main theme, though the matters with which they deal are of great importance. Chapter XI (Foreign Trade), treating briefly a subject which requires a volume to itself, shows how the matters which we have been discussing from the point of view of the world appear differently when we look at them from the point of view of a single country. Chapter XII (Changes in Employment) gathers the various pieces together and provides a picture of the oscillations of employment in the modern economic system.

Certain controversial points are discussed in the course of the argument (particularly in the Appendixes, to Chapter X on the Quantity Theory of Money and to Chapter XI on Free Trade), but as far as possible controversy has been avoided. Some reflections on economic controversy are put forward in the last chapter.

CHAPTER II

INVESTMENT AND SAVING

TERMINOLOGY

THE concept of *investment* plays an important part in the argument which follows, and it is necessary at the outset to be clear about terms. By *investment* is meant an addition to real capital, such as occurs when a new house or a new factory is built, a railway line constructed or a store of raw materials accumulated. This use of the word does not correspond to the everyday sense in which investment means merely acquiring a title to capital. In ordinary speech we may say " I have invested £100 in Home Rails ", but in the present context " investment " does not mean buying a piece of paper, but making an addition to the stock of goods in existence. You are not investing when you buy a security ; you are investing when you cause a house to be built.

The word saving, on the other hand, is used in its ordinary sense. Saving is the difference between income and expenditure upon current consumption. *Income* also is used in its everyday sense. Refined complications have been raised in connection with the definition of these terms, but for our present purposes a rough-and-ready treatment will suffice.

All income is derived ultimately from selling goods and services. It may be derived by working for wages or salaries, or from owning property, land or capital equipment, which contributes to the output of goods, or from lending money, in which case interest is paid out of receipts derived from selling goods and services, or from gifts or allowances from people who derive income from one of these sources. All income, therefore, is derived either from providing for current consumption or from adding to the stock of wealth, that is, from investment. The work of repairing and renewing existing capital goods is best regarded as part of the process of producing consumption goods, and incomes derived from such activities must not be reckoned as investment incomes.

EQUALITY OF INVESTMENT AND SAVING

We have already seen that an individual who adds to his private wealth by saving, that is, by consuming less than the whole of his income, does nothing to encourage the production of more real capital, in short that saving in itself does not cause investment to take place. But yet it can easily be seen that for the community as a whole the rate of saving must be equal to the rate of investment. All incomes are derived either from producing consumption goods or from producing investment goods. And all income either is spent on consumption goods or is saved. The income derived from producing consumption goods is equal to what is spent on them. Therefore what is saved is equal to the income derived from producing investment goods. In short, the rate of saving is equal to the rate of investment.

$S = I$ (N)

To look at the same thing in another way : each individual who saves adds to his wealth, while any individual who spends more than his income — that is, dis-saves — reduces his wealth, either by getting rid of part of his past accumulation or by increasing his indebtedness. The sum of all the savings, positive and negative, of individuals is the total increase in wealth of the community, and

7

the increase in wealth of the community, over any period, is the investment which has taken place in that period.

But saving is not the same thing as investment. To say that the rate of saving is equal to the rate of investment, for all individuals taken together, does not mean that each individual act of saving leads to a corresponding act of investment. Every individual is free to spend or save his income just as he pleases. His motives for saving are governed by such influences as prudence, family feeling, pride, or inability to think of a new way of spending money. At the same time every entrepreneur is free to decide how much it is worth while to invest in creating new capital goods, having regard to the prospects of profit. Decisions to save and decisions to invest are taken quite independently of each other, and for a quite different class of motives.

In some individual cases the two decisions are bound together, as when a man cuts down his consumption in order to save up and have a house built for himself. But normally even private building is done out of borrowing or out of accumulated wealth, not at the expense of current consumption. Again, in a society different from our own the decision to save and the decision to invest in creating new capital goods may be tied together. Under a completely socialist system the government would decide how much investment was desirable, and would control the amount of collective saving accordingly. Or, in a primitive community, with no money and no borrowing, saving can only take the form of adding to the stock of goods owned by the individual family. When the family desire to save more, they eat up less of the year's crop and retain a larger stock in their barns.

But in the system under which we live the decision to save and the decision to invest are not bound together, and the motives governing them are quite different. How then does it come about that, on balance, individuals always decide to save just as much as entrepreneurs have decided to invest ?

WHAT HAPPENS WHEN INVESTMENT INCREASES

Let us suppose that in a time of general unemployment entrepreneurs decide to extend their plant at a greater rate than formerly, while the desire of individuals to save remains the same. An increase in activity now takes place in the capital-good industries. Incomes increase — men formerly unemployed begin to receive wages and profits go up. Part of these additional incomes are spent, activity in the consumption-good industries also increases, and a further increase in incomes takes place.

Now, with a higher level of income, and the same general attitude to saving as before, the amount that people save will increase. For without any change in the general state of family affection, foresight and pride — without, that is to say, any change in the desire to save — people will save more when their incomes are higher. A change in the desire to save means that people are inclined to save more out of the same income. But with the same desire to save, the actual amount of saving will depend upon the income they have to dispose of. As the most urgent needs are met, and the standard of life becomes more comfortable, the importance of present consumption grows less compared to the advantages of owning wealth, and the moral effort of refraining from present consumption becomes less strenuous. Thus, as a general rule, saving increases with income. This rule does not apply to every individual, nor to any one individual in all circumstances, but, as we should expect, it is found to hold good by and large.

9

Saving depends upon income, and income depends upon the rate at which investment goods are being produced. Everyone is free to save as much as he likes, but how much he likes to save is influenced by his income, and his income is influenced by the decisions of entrepreneurs as to how much it is worth their while to invest. Thus everyone does what he likes, but what he likes is determined for him by the entrepreneurs. Saving is equal to investment, because investment leads to a state of affairs in which people want to save. Investment causes incomes to be whatever is required to induce people to save at a rate equal to the rate of investment. The more willing people are to save, the lower is the level of income corresponding to a given rate of investment, and the smaller the increase in income brought about by a given increase in the rate of investment.

What Happens when the Desire to Save Increases

The argument does not run in the reverse way. The desire to save does not promote investment. Let us suppose that individuals' desire to save increases — that is, the amount they will save out of a given income goes up — while entrepreneurs are undertaking investment at the same rate as before. Then, some individuals will spend less of their income than formerly. Activity and income in the consumption-good trades will therefore fall off. Owing to this decline in income, consumption will be further curtailed, and a further decline in incomes will take place. One man's expenditure is other men's income, and when one man spends less, other men earn less. As incomes fall the amount that individuals want to save is cut down, and income for the community as a whole is reduced to the level at which the actual rate of saving is no greater than the rate of investment. The more reluctant people are to cut down their saving, the greater will be the fall in incomes.

Thus we see once more that whatever the attitude of individuals to saving may be, the amount that they will actually save, taken together, is determined for them by the decisions of the entrepreneurs as to the amount of investment goods that it suits them to produce. Any one individual, it is true, can increase his rate of saving, but the very fact that he is saving more, which means that he is spending less, leads to a decline in other people's incomes to such an extent that they save less, and his saving makes no change in the total rate of saving. The individual saver has no direct influence upon the rate of investment. If entrepreneurs see a profit to be made by investment, investment will take place, and if they do not it will not. The initiative lies with the entrepreneurs, not with the savers. The savers, as a group, are helpless in the hands of the entrepreneurs, though any one individually is free to save as much as he likes. If the desire of individuals to save increases, but the desire of entrepreneurs to create new capital goods does not increase, then no increase in the rate of aggregate saving can take place and the impulse to save runs to waste. Consumption falls off, and incomes decline as much as consumption, so that in spite of the sacrifices of increased thrift no increase in saving takes place ; abstinence brings no reward of added wealth to the community. The actions and decisions of the savers can have no direct effect upon the rate at which new capital goods are created. All that they can influence directly is the level of current consumption and current output of consumption goods, and so the level of income and total activity.

The "Hoarding" Fallacy

Some writers appear to disagree with this view. Savings, they say, are devoted to buying securities, and if saving increases there is an increased demand for securities. New securities are issued in order to finance investment, and therefore an increase in saving leads to an increase in investment. This argument sinks at the first step, for, since an individual, by increasing his own savings, reduces the savings of others, he does not add to the rate of saving of the community, and therefore does not add to the demand for securities. But the initial error leads to a further complication. If saving directly caused investment, it would be very difficult to see how unemployment could possibly occur, and such writers, in order to provide an explanation of unemployment, usually fall back on the notion of "hoarding". If an individual saves, they say, and buys securities with his new wealth, investment automatically increases, but if he puts his new wealth into money, that is, hoards it, there is no corresponding investment. But this is simply an error. The saving of the individual is not a cause of investment in either case, and the distinction does not arise. We shall find, it is true, that the desire of individuals to hold their wealth (whether newly saved or owned for some time makes no difference) in money rather than securities plays an important part in influencing the rate of investment, *via* the rate of interest. But this is an indirect and complicated effect. The individual saver has no direct influence on the rate of investment, whether he buys securities or not. He may buy securities or add to his holding of money, whichever he pleases, but since other people are saving less because he is saving more they are buying less securities or parting with money they formerly held. The question of how wealth is held, whether in money or securities, has only the slightest connection with the interaction of investment and saving.

The error connected with the idea of "hoarding" arises, no doubt, from the desire to find where the vanished savings have got to. It is clear enough that if the desire of individuals to save has increased, but the desire of entrepreneurs to invest has not increased, then actually savings do not increase, and the explanation is put forward that the missing savings have somehow got lost on the way by going into money instead of into securities. But this is not a tenable explanation. The savings are nowhere. They have failed to come into existence, because as fast as one man increases his saving, by reducing his spending, other men's incomes fall off and they save less as much as he saves more. It is of no use to search for the non-existent savings either in "hoards" or anywhere else.

SUMMARY

To sum up : When investment increases, incomes rise to the point at which saving increases equally, but if the desire to save increases, incomes fall off so much that on balance saving is no greater than before. It is through changes in income that the equality of saving and investment is preserved. Thus the level of income is determined by the rate of investment and the desire to save ; given the desire to save, the level of income that will rule is governed by the rate of investment. And given the rate of investment the level of income is determined by the desire to save.

We are now able to give a provisional account of how it comes about that resources can be wasted in idleness. If the amount that entrepreneurs in given conditions are willing to invest is less than the amount that individuals, taken together, would want to save out of the incomes which the full employment of resources would entail, then there cannot be full employment, and incomes will in fact be less than they would be if full employment obtained. Or to look at the same thing in another way — suppose that the investment decisions of entrepreneurs have been taken, in the light of expected future profit. Then the current rate of investment is given, and if individuals are not willing to spend on current consumption the whole difference between the rate of investment and the total of income that there would be if there were full employment, then there will not be full employment.

Thus the popular description of unemployment as " poverty in the midst of plenty " contains a large element of truth, for in one sense unemployment arises because the incomes which some individuals would enjoy, in the absence of unemployment, would be so large that they would not want to spend enough money to make it profitable for entrepreneurs to give everyone employment who wants to work.

This is merely a provisional account of matters which will become clearer as our argument proceeds.

CHAPTER III

THE MULTIPLIER

PRIMARY AND SECONDARY EMPLOYMENT

WE must now consider in more detail the effect of an increase in investment upon income and upon saving. When an increase in investment takes place, say in house-building, at a time of general unemployment, men are given jobs in building, in making materials, such as bricks, glass and door-knobs, and in transport. The additional employment thus given is the *primary* increase in employment due to the increase in investment. When employment increases the men concerned increase their rate of consumption — buying more boots and shirts and bacon and cheese. Similarly, when more profits are being made by building contractors and so forth, the individuals whose incomes have increased will spend more upon con-sumption goods. Thus employment will increase, and more profits will be earned, in making the boots and other goods for which the market has now improved. The boot operatives, in turn, have more money to spend when they are taken into work, shareholders receive larger dividends, the shops and cinemas and garages make bigger profits. With larger incomes being earned in the con-sumption-good industries a further increase in consump-tion takes place, and employment and profits, in making boots and selling petrol and the rest, increase still further. Larger incomes again lead to more consumption, and so on round and round. The addition to employment in the consumption-good industries is the *secondary* increase in employment due to the increase in investment.

At each round the addition to employment and to incomes is less than at the last. The receiver of profits increases his rate of saving when his income increases, so that less than the whole of the additional profits earned at each round is used to increase consumption. And only a part of the wage which a man receives when he finds work is an addition to his income. Even when he was unemployed he was not living on air. He may have been receiving unemployment benefit, relief payments, or assistance from friends or from charity, or he may have kept body and soul together by drawing on his own past accumulated savings, by pawning his furniture or getting into debt to shopkeepers. For convenience we will describe the income of the unemployed, from whatever source it may be drawn, as *dole* income. Part of the expenditure which a man makes when he earns wages merely replaces the dole which he was spending while he was unemployed. Thus less than the whole outlay upon house-building is passed on to the consumption-good industries at the second round and less than the whole of the additional incomes received at the second round is passed on at the third round, and so forth.

The extent to which income is passed on from round to round governs the increase in employment. The ratio of the total increase in employment to the primary increase is known as the *Multiplier*. If, for example, there is an increase in employment of two men in consumption-good industries for every man newly employed in capital-good industries, then the Multiplier is equal to 3.

SAVING EQUATED TO INVESTMENT

The very fact that the whole increase of income is not passed on at each round means that at each round there is an increase in the rate of saving. First, there is an increase of saving out of profits at each stage. Secondly, a reduction in dole payments leads to an increase in saving or decrease in dis-saving. Part or the whole of unemployment relief may be financed by borrowing by the state, and if the state is spending more than it is receiving from taxes, and borrowing the difference, the effect is exactly the same as if an individual is spending more than his income and so reducing his wealth or increasing his indebtedness. When the dole is provided from taxation, so that a reduction in dole payments leads to a remission of taxes, saving by taxpayers increases when a decline in dole payments reduces the burden of taxation. Part of the dole may come from dis-saving or borrowing by the unemployed themselves or by their friends, and charitable individuals may save more when claims upon them are reduced. Thus, one way and another, a reduction in dole payments leads to a reduction in dis-saving or an increase in saving.

It is obvious that, whatever happens, the increase in saving which people, taken together, are induced to make when their incomes are increased as a result of the greater rate of house-building, must be equal to the increased outlay on house-building. For whatever is not saved is spent. If the whole of the outlay on house-building were added to saving at the first round, there would be no second round. In so far as the individuals directly concerned in the house-building increase their consumption, they increase their rate of saving by less than their incomes have increased, that is, by less than the outlay on house-building. But precisely because they do not increase their savings as much as their income has increased, they cause an increase in the incomes, and consequently the savings, of the people concerned in making additional goods for them to consume. And in so far as these people, in turn, save less than the whole addition to their incomes, they cause the incomes of others to increase. Thus the increase in incomes must necessarily continue up to the point at which there is an addition to saving equal to the additional outlay on house-building.

EXAMPLES

To take a simplified example, let us suppose (1) that half of all incomes is wage incomes, and the other half profits ; (2) that out of an addition to profits one-third is saved ; (3) that the whole of wages is spent upon consumption goods ; (4) that the dole of an unemployed man is equal to one-third of the wage of an employed man ; (5) that the whole of dole incomes is provided by borrowing. Then for every additional £1 per week spent upon house-building, wages at the first round are increased by £$\frac{1}{2}$ per week, and profits by £$\frac{1}{2}$. The consumption of wage earners is increased by $\frac{2}{3}$ of the wage, that is, by £$\frac{1}{3}$; and consumption by the recipients of profits is increased by £$\frac{1}{3}$. Thus incomes at the second round are increased by £$\frac{2}{3}$, the additional expenditure coming from those whose incomes are increased at the first round. Wages at the second round are increased by £$\frac{1}{3}$, profits by £$\frac{1}{3}$, and expenditure on consumption goods by £$\frac{4}{9}$; and so forth.

Thus for every £1 per week added to outlay on house-building there is an addition to income, for the community as a whole, of

$$£1 + \tfrac{2}{3} + \tfrac{4}{9} + \tfrac{8}{27} + \ldots ., \quad \text{a total of £3 per week,}$$

and for every man newly employed in house-building, 2 men are given employment in the consumption-good industries. In this example the Multiplier is 3, that is to say, the total increase in employment is three times the primary increase in employment in building and providing housing materials.

For every £1 per week spent on house-building there is a reduction, at the first round, of £$\frac{1}{3}$ in dole payments, and an increase of £$\frac{1}{3}$ in saving from profits. We are supposing that the whole of the dole represents dis-saving. Thus there is a net increase in saving, at the first round, of £$\frac{1}{3}$. £$\frac{2}{3}$ of additional income at the second round reduces dole payments by £$\frac{1}{3}$, and causes saving out of profits to increase by £$\frac{1}{3}$, and so on. Thus the total increase in net saving per week is equal to

$$£\tfrac{1}{3}(1) + \tfrac{1}{3}(\tfrac{2}{3}) + \tfrac{1}{3}(\tfrac{4}{9}) + \ldots, \quad \text{a total of £1 per week.}$$

Thus for every £1 added to outlay on house-building £1 is added to saving.

To take another example, suppose that part of wages is saved, let us say one-sixth (that is, a quarter of the difference between the wage and the dole), and that half of the addition to profits is saved. The series for income now becomes

$$£1 + \tfrac{1}{2} + \tfrac{1}{4} + \tfrac{1}{8} + \ldots, \quad \text{and the Multiplier is 2.}$$

Once more saving is increased pound for pound with the increase in investment, for the series for saving now becomes

$$£\tfrac{1}{2}(1) + \tfrac{1}{2}(\tfrac{1}{2}) + \tfrac{1}{2}(\tfrac{1}{4}) + \ldots, \quad \text{a total of £1.}$$

Thus we find, as we have already seen, that however willing or reluctant the community may be to save, the rate of saving is always equal to the rate of investment. Greater willingness to save checks the increase in incomes, and reduces the size of the Multiplier, but it cannot increase the saving that is brought about by an increase in investment.

THE SIZE OF THE MULTIPLIER

We are now able to see the main influences which determine the size of the Multiplier. The Multiplier will be larger the smaller is the addition to saving made from an addition to profits (a third of additional profits in our first example, and half in our second). And since wages are more fully spent than profits, the Multiplier will be larger the greater is the ratio of wages to profits (half in both examples). Only the difference between the wage and the dole is added to the income of a worker when he finds employment, and the lower the ratio of the dole to the wage (a third in both examples) the larger will be the Multiplier tend to be.

In our first example we assumed that the whole of wages is spent, in the second that one-sixth is saved. Saving out of wages depends very much upon the immediate past history of the families concerned. An unemployed man may keep body and soul together partly by getting into debt, by drawing on past accumulations or by pawning his goods. When he finds work he will want to pay off his debts, store up his nest-egg again and redeem his pledges. As time goes by, debts are paid off and expenditure tends to increase. This is one reason, amongst many, why we should not expect the value of the Multiplier to be the same at all times. Its value depends upon the particular situation at the moment when investment increases, and if a steady rate of investment is kept up over a period of time the total of employment will gradually alter.

It is also necessary to consider the manner in which dole payments are provided for. In our examples we assumed that they were entirely financed by borrowing. If the dole which an unemployed man receives comes from the income of other people, whether through taxation or from charity, then those people are likely to increase their own consumption when they are relieved from the necessity of providing for the unemployed. Thus the Multiplier will be larger if the dole is financed by taxation which is remitted when unemployment is reduced than if it is financed entirely by borrowing.

THE MULTIPLIER IN ONE COUNTRY

We have so far discussed the Multiplier from the point of view of the world as a whole. If we are interested only in the increase in employment in the home country when investment at home increases, we must make an allowance for imports. When employment at home increases, and expenditure on consumption goods goes up, part of this increase in expenditure will fall on foreign-produced goods, and part of the secondary increase in employment, due to the investment at home, will take place outside the home country. If the newly employed bricklayer buys foreign boots, part of the secondary employment and secondary profits, due to house-building in Cambridge, goes to Czecho-Slovakia instead of to Northampton, and when he buys a shirt, part of the secondary employment and profits go to America, where the raw cotton is grown. Thus the Multiplier for one country alone is smaller than the Multiplier for the world as a whole.

The actual value of the Multiplier, in particular countries in particular circumstances, is a matter of great interest and importance. Two methods can be used to estimate it. One, illustrated in our examples (though these were highly simplified), is to form a reasonable guess at the magnitudes involved, the ratio of wages to profits, of the dole to the wage, of saving to profits, and so forth, and to work out the appropriate geometrical progression. The other method is to study actual changes in employment in capital-good industries and in industry in general and discover the ratio between them. These methods are both being used, and have been found to give reasonably consonant results. It appears that in a period of depression, such as 1931 to 1935 in this country, the Multiplier was round about 2, while, as we should expect, the Multiplier for the U.S.A., which is much less dependent upon imports, was considerably larger.

CHAPTER IV

CHANGES IN INVESTMENT

THE INDUCEMENT TO INVEST

WE have seen that the rate of investment plays an essential part in determining the level of employment and incomes at any moment. What determines the rate of investment? Once more we shall consider the problem from the point of view of the world as a whole. The question of investment in a single country will be treated later.

Entrepreneurs acquire capital goods with a view to using them to produce consumption goods or other capital goods which can be sold at a profit, and the main considerations which govern the demand for them are their expected future earnings and the ruling rate of interest. If the expected earnings of a machine reckoned as a percentage on its cost, allowing for expenses of upkeep and for risk, works out at more than the ruling rate of interest, then there will be a demand for that sort of machine, for it will be profitable to borrow money and order the machine. In the main the same considerations govern the purchase of a machine out of a firm's own resources, for it is folly to sacrifice the interest which would be earned on a sum of money by lending it or holding securities with it, in order to purchase a machine which will earn less. Thus the rate of investment is governed by prospective profits compared to the rate of interest.

To look at the same thing in another way, the price of existing capital goods is determined by their expected earnings and the rate of interest, and it will be profitable to produce new capital goods so long as their cost of production does not exceed this price. Suppose that a certain type of house in a certain town can be let for £60 a year, of which £10 must be spent on upkeep to maintain it permanently in good repair. Then the net earnings of the house is £50 a year. When the rate of interest is 5 per cent. this house is worth £1000, for no one will give more (or accept less) than £1000 for something which yields an income of £50 a year when £50 a year can be obtained as interest on £1000. At 6 per cent. the house is worth £833, at 4 per cent. £1250. Now, if such a house costs £1000 to build, it will be just worth while to build new houses of this type when the rate of interest is 5 per cent. If the rate of interest were 6 per cent. no more such houses would be built, while if the rate of interest were 4 per cent. a building boom would set in. The rate of interest is thus an extremely important influence upon investment. What determines the rate of interest will be discussed in a later chapter.

PROSPECTIVE PROFITS

Estimates of the future earnings of capital goods must, in the nature of the case, be based largely upon guess-work, and investment will increase if, for any reason, expectations of future earnings of capital goods become more cheerful. Thus a revival of confidence as to the future state of trade has an extremely important effect in promoting investment. We here catch a glimpse of one of the causes of the instability of a system of private enterprise. For the current level of demand for consumption goods is an important influence upon the prospective earnings of capital equipment. But an increase in the rate at which capital goods are being produced itself, as we have seen, raises the demand for consumption goods. Thus any upward or downward movement in activity tends to amplify itself up to a certain point.

The prospective earnings of capital goods also depend upon the amount in existence. If an earthquake suddenly destroys part of a city the houses which remain standing become more valuable, and there will be a profit to be made by building new houses. The same principle is at work, in a milder way, in normal times. If slump conditions have been so bad that it has not seemed worth while even to renew old equipment as it wears out, then one fine day entrepreneurs will wake up to the fact that the old equipment which remains has become more valuable, and new equipment will begin to be ordered. Conversely, as capital accumulates more and more equipment is competing to satisfy a demand for consumption goods, and the rate of profit on capital falls off.

Thus there is a rhythmical tendency in investment. When slump conditions have continued for a certain time investment begins to revive. The mere fact that investment has begun to increase raises the level of activity and so fires the hope of future profit from investment. The upward movement continues to feed upon itself until the accumulation of capital depresses the rate of profit. Hope turns to pessimism and a downward movement begins, which will once more reverse itself after a certain time has elapsed.

So long as population is increasing, new inventions are constantly being made, and new territories opened up to trade, the demand for capital goods is constantly expanding, independently of the rhythmical rise and fall of activity. In such conditions slumps will be less severe and will come to an end more quickly than when population and technical knowledge are stable. It is mainly for this reason that unemployment was a less serious problem in the nineteenth century than it is to-day. For in the nineteenth century the western economic world was expanding in every way, so that the demand for new capital was always running ahead faster than investment could catch up upon it, and prospective profits never fell very low, or remained low for very long.

Public Investment

A large amount of investment, in such things as improvements in roads, school buildings, extensions of telephone equipment, playing-fields, gas-works and so forth, is undertaken by the state and local authorities. These are not subject to the profit motive in the same direct way as private investment, and do not necessarily follow the same rhythm. Some of them, such as a municipal gas-works, yield a money return, but others, such as recreation grounds, are undertaken with a view to a benefit to the community which does not show itself directly in money receipts. Another kind of state investment is the provision of armaments.

All these kinds of investment produce an immediate effect, while incomes are being earned in constructing the capital works, upon the current demand for consumption goods, which is of exactly the same nature as that produced by investment undertaken by profit-seeking entrepreneurs. The immediate effect upon employment of a scheme of investment is nothing whatever to do with the usefulness or earning-power of the capital goods produced. When the Tower of Babel was being built a large number of men were engaged upon an entirely unproductive enterprise, but while they were at work they had to be clothed and fed ; their wages were spent upon the current output of consumption-good industries, which must have enjoyed a boom while the building was going on, and suffered a violent slump when the project was abandoned.

It is of course always desirable on general grounds that employment in the capital-good industries should be turned to the best advantage and be used for making valuable capital goods, which will add to future wealth, instead of being used for foolish projects, but the immediate effect upon employment is in no way enhanced by the future usefulness of the capital works. This is a fact which the public in general find it somewhat hard to grasp. There is a strong moral resistance against believing that a piece of investment that is useless, or even harmful, in its long-run aspect, can be beneficial in the sense of increasing employment and income while it is going on. But there is no getting away from the fact that employment will be increased when investment increases, whether the investment is useful or not. The application of this argument to investment in armaments is obvious.

Now, when unemployment is rife, the cost to a government of a given piece of investment — say, building a road — is very much less than the actual outlay made upon the road. For when employment increases, in road-building, in quarrying to provide materials, and in consumption-good industries catering for the extra expenditure of individuals engaged in road-building and quarrying, the responsibility of the government and local authorities for unemployment allowances is thereby reduced. Moreover, when activity increases the yield of taxes goes up. Incomes are higher, and more income tax is paid, more tea and beer and cigarettes are consumed. With the same rates of taxes as before the receipts of the Exchequer go up. It is calculated that, one way and another, something like half of the outlay upon public works comes directly back to the government, even when allowance is made for the leakage of secondary employment to foreign countries. Thus to finance a scheme of, say, £100 million the government has to add to its borrowing only £50 million.

This in itself provides a strong argument, from the government point of view, for pressing forward with public works schemes when unemployment exists. Suppose that the rate of interest is 3 per cent. Then any scheme which is reckoned to yield 1½ per cent. on its initial cost, either in direct money receipts (for instance, the rent received from a state housing scheme) or in indirect benefits (for instance, the advantages of having better roads), is a sound investment even from a narrow commercial point of view.

This is one of the most striking instances of a divergence between individual and social advantages. Any private entrepreneur who decides to undertake investment is benefiting his fellow entrepreneurs and the government, by causing an increase in incomes, in consumption and in tax payments. But the private entrepreneur feels no benefit from the additional incomes which his action causes other people to earn, and if he is borrowing at 3 per cent. he must see at least a 3 per cent. return on his outlay. Thus a government has strong motives for undertaking investment which the private entrepreneur does not feel.

But this is not the end of the story. When investment takes place, then, as we have seen, incomes are increased to such an extent that saving is increased as much as investment. Thus private individuals add to their wealth sums equal to the additional government borrowing, and this they retain as a permanent possession. Interest on a government loan has to be paid out of taxation, and if the

National Debt increases tax payments have to increase to provide interest. But the taxpayers, taken together, are precisely the same people as the interest receivers. Their wealth, in their capacity as owners of capital, has gone up exactly as much as their liabilities, in their capacity as taxpayers responsible for the National Debt. Thus, except for a certain nuisance-cost of collecting additional taxes (which may, it is true, become important if the National Debt is very large), the community as a whole is no worse off for the extra government borrowing. Even if the public works were quite useless in themselves they still would not constitute any expense to the community as a whole ; while the community would enjoy the benefits of a higher level of employment, income and consumption while the works were being carried out.

To look at the same thing in another way, when there is unemployment resources are idle. The only real cost of setting them to work is a reduction in undesired idleness. Any addition to the real capital of the country resulting from public works, however great or small it may be, is a pure gain ; and over and above the permanent gain of real capital there is the temporary gain of increased consumption and diminished misery which occurs as long as the schemes are being carried out. The idea that public works can be " wasteful ", in a time of severe unemployment, is therefore an illusion. It would be wasteful to undertake foolish projects instead of sensible ones, but it is not wasteful to undertake even foolish projects instead of none at all. For if none are undertaken, resources are wasted in idleness, and nothing is saved by not doing the works.

It thus appears that when private entrepreneurs are not undertaking sufficient investment to provide a high level of employment, governments have a strong motive to increase investment in public works. During the years of severe depression following 1929, governments have been acting increasingly on this view. This country has been somewhat exceptional, and British governments have on the whole allowed themselves to be swayed by the same sentiments as private entrepreneurs — increasing public works just when trade is improving, and indulging in so-called economy just when unemployment begins to increase. But, the world over, governments have begun to realise that they can help to prevent fluctuations in employment by increasing public works when private investment falls off. Public works therefore act to some extent as a counterweight to the fluctuations in investment undertaken by profit-seeking entrepreneurs.

INVESTMENT IN WORKING CAPITAL AND STOCKS

Two special kinds of investment must also be considered. These are investment in working capital and investment in stocks of goods. When output is increasing, working capital, that is, the value of goods in process, must increase. As soon as the output has settled down to a new higher level the investment in working capital comes to an end. When you are starting to make sausages you begin by putting some meat into the back of the sausage machine, and for a few minutes, as you turn the handle, nothing comes out at the front. Meanwhile the amount of meat in the machine is increasing. After a time sausage meat begins to come out at the front at the same rate as you are putting it in at the back, and the amount of meat in the machine ceases to increase. Similarly, when you decide to stop, for a certain time after you have ceased to put meat in at the back it continues to come out at the front, and meanwhile the amount of meat in the machine is falling off, until finally the machine becomes empty.

Any change in the rate of output of industry leads to investment or disinvestment in working capital, and the effect upon employment of investment in working capital is the same as the effect of investment in capital goods. Men are paid wages for starting to produce goods before the goods are ready for sale, and expenditure from their wages falls upon goods already becoming available. Thus there is a special kind of investment which is made for a certain period after the decision has been taken to increase output, and this is an important reason why any influence towards an increase in output tends to amplify itself up to a certain point.

Investment in stocks of goods, on the other hand, acts rather as a counterweight to other forms of investment. When demand is falling off dealers may prefer to accumulate stocks of non-perishable commodities, such as wheat or metals, rather than to sell them at a loss, so that for a time increased investment in stocks partly counterbalances diminished investment in durable capital goods and in working capital. Similarly, when trade begins to revive goods are taken from stocks to be sold, and while stocks are falling, a given increase in expenditure upon consumption goods leads to a correspondingly smaller increase in the rate of output of new consumption goods.

These two movements, changes in working capital and changes in stocks, come into play when output, for other reasons, is in the course of changing. They may be of considerable importance, but are not likely by themselves to initiate a change in activity.

CHAPTER V

CHANGES IN THRIFTINESS

THE SCHEDULE OF THRIFTINESS

WE have seen already that a change in the desire to save is powerless to alter the actual amount of saving done by the community as a whole, for the actual rate of saving is determined by the rate of investment which is being undertaken. But the desire to save has an important influence on the level of incomes. If I decide to save £1 a week more than formerly, the shopkeepers and manufacturers who had been supplying my wants now receive £1 a week less than before. Consequently they must either save less or spend less. In so far as they spend less, other incomes are reduced, and so on round and round. Thus the reduction in my expenditure by £1 a week leads to a fall in incomes to such a point that the savings of other people are reduced by £1 per week. If the Multiplier is 3, the reduction in my expenditure by £1 a week will cause a fall in income of £3 per week. After, say, a year I shall have added £52 to my wealth, but others will be poorer by £52 than they would have been if I had not saved that sum. Thus for all of us taken together wealth has not increased, but income has declined.

In short, the rate of investment determines the rate of saving, and given the rate of investment, the desire to save determines the level of incomes. By the desire to save, or *thriftiness* of the community, we mean the whole complex of influences which determine how much will be saved at each level of income. The thriftiness of an individual is represented by a schedule of the amount he would save at each level of income, and the thriftiness of the community is represented by the total of saving corresponding to each level of total income. For this country a small section of the schedule of thriftiness is something like this :

£ Million	
Income	Saving
4300	280
4600	420
4800	550

% ↑ as income increases

Given the schedule of thriftiness the level of income depends upon the rate of investment. Thus, in the above example, if investment is being carried out at a rate of £420 million per year, income will be £4600 million per year. With a lower rate of investment, income would be lower, with a higher rate higher. The level of income is always such as to equate the rate of saving to the rate of investment.

THE INFLUENCE OF THE STOCK EXCHANGE

Changes in thriftiness may accompany the ups and downs of trade. An improved state of confidence about the future may not only lead entrepreneurs to invest more but also may lead individuals to spend more, for as the weather improves the fear of a rainy day grows less acute.

There is a special reason for expecting this sort of thing to happen. When trade improves the prospects of industrial concerns of all sorts look brighter, and precisely the same capital assets are valued by the public at a higher figure, because confidence in their future earning and dividend-paying power has gone up. In short, there is a boom on the Stock Exchange. Now any individual who happened to have bought some shares before the boom began finds that their value has risen, that is to say, if he sold them now he would get more for them than he paid. He may not want to sell, but the fact that he *could* sell at a high figure gives him a comfortable sensation and makes him feel rich. He is therefore less stern in denying himself expenditure on consumption of all sorts, and his rate of saving goes down.

The original Stock Exchange boom was a consequence of the increase in prospective profits, which both results from and further promotes an increase in investment. On top of this the Stock Exchange boom promotes increased consumption. Thus there is an increase in the rate of consumption corresponding to a given rate of investment at the same time as investment itself is increasing. The upswing of activity, employment and profits therefore tends to magnify itself. This phenomenon was of great importance during the great Wall Street boom which ended in 1929. It is probably also at work in a milder way whenever there is a marked rise in Stock Exchange prices.

A Budget Deficit

A special kind of reduction in thriftiness is represented by a budget deficit. If the state is paying out more money in salaries to civil servants, commissions to contractors and so forth, than it is receiving in taxation, and is borrowing the difference by issuing Treasury bills or otherwise raising loans from the public, then it is in just the same position as an individual who is spending on current consumption more than his income, by means of drawing on past accumulated wealth or getting into debt. In short the state is dis-saving. The result is to increase incomes and expenditure all round. Suppose that the state keeps its outlay constant and remits taxation. Then out of the increased net income of taxpayers part will be spent, and this extra spending will raise the incomes of those on whose output the expenditure is made. Out of this extra income, again, a part will be spent; and so on. Just as in the case of investment, the extra expenditure will lead to such an increase in incomes that the public are saving more than they otherwise would have done at just the same rate as the government is borrowing.

The idea that a budget deficit is good for trade is often found to be shocking, but it is a fact which has become obvious to the governments of the world since the great depression began in 1929. The argument used to be common, particularly in England, that a budget deficit upsets the confidence of entrepreneurs, and so does more indirect harm to employment than direct good. But this is a case where " thinking makes it so ", and it is found nowadays that a deficit accompanied by the right sort of propaganda can have a very beneficial effect.

The mere fact that a deficit is good for trade is not a sufficient argument for having a deficit, since other methods of improving trade may be preferable. It can, however, be regarded as a merciful dispensation that budgets have a tendency to come unstuck when trade is very bad. Taxes fail to yield as much as was expected, while expenses in connection with unemployment go up, and the government is forced to borrow to meet its current outgoings. This has the effect of preventing the decline in employment from going so far as it would if the budget were kept balanced.

✳ INEQUALITY OF INCOMES ✕

An important influence upon the thriftiness of the community is the distribution of a given total income amongst individuals. Generally speaking, the more unequally is income distributed the greater will be the thriftiness of the community. If £100 a year is taken away from a man with £10,000 a year, he will not alter his standard of life very much, but will reduce his rate of saving. But if £100 a year is given to a man who had £150 before, his standard of life will certainly be raised to very nearly the full extent of the extra income. Thus taking the two men together the transfer will increase the amount of consumption out of their combined income of £10,150. We have already seen this principle at work in the determination of the Multiplier, for we found that a given increment of income will lead to a greater increment of saving the more of that increment of income goes to profits and the less to wages.

The general psychological attitude to saving, depending upon family affection, prudence, self-control and so forth, being unaltered, thriftiness will be reduced if measures are taken to reduce the inequality of income. Suppose that the tax system is altered in such a way that a larger amount of taxes is paid by the richest part of the community and a smaller amount by the poorest. The net income of the richest class is now reduced. They will cut down their expenditure to some extent, but not to the full extent of the additional taxation. On the other hand the increased net incomes of the poorest class will be devoted almost entirely to increased consumption. Thus the amount saved out of a given total income will be reduced, while increased expenditure will bring about an increase in the total of income, so that the actual amount of saving is no less than before.

It has sometimes been argued that the fact that inequality of incomes promotes thriftiness is a justification for inequality, and it is held to be highly dangerous to tax the rich for the benefit of the poor on the ground that it will dry up the source from which capital accumulation comes. Even on its own ground this argument is very unconvincing. It is an extremely uneconomic method of getting saving done to fatten up a certain number of people to the point at which saving is no effort to them, and if it is held to be the justification of high incomes that they are partly saved, then all that part which is spent in providing the rich with a luxurious standard of life must be regarded as pure waste. Moreover, there is no reason to suppose that the degree of thriftiness which results from inequality of incomes corresponds to the desirability of saving from a social point of view. It would be the height of folly for a man to ruin his health by starvation in the present in order to accumulate wealth for the future, and it is hard to contend, in existing circumstances, that a more rapid rate of capital accumulation is to be preferred to a higher standard of life for the poorest part of the community.

But however that may be, the attempt to justify inequality because it promotes thriftiness falls to the ground as soon as we realise that an increase in thriftiness does not by itself cause an increase in capital accumulation to take place.

THRIFT AS A SOCIAL VIRTUE

Thriftiness does not cause investment to take place, but at the same time it is thriftiness which makes investment possible. There is always an upper limit to the expansion of output, set by the resources available. The more thrifty people are, that is, the less they are inclined to consume, the more resources are left over from providing for current consumption, and these resources (given time to transfer men, and adapt land and machinery, from one use to another) are available to be used for investment. When the motive for investment is weak the resources run to waste in idleness, and we are inclined to regard a reduction of thriftiness as a benefit to society. If these resources are not being used to accumulate capital for the future, we say, let us at least enjoy what we can by eating up their products in the present. But when the motive for investment is strong the whole matter appears in a different light. When the rate of investment is pressing against the limit set by available resources, and all workers are fully employed, then no further increase in the rate of investment can take place unless consumption declines, and an increase in consumption, in such circumstances, instead of setting idle resources to work, can only be made at the expense of investment.

In an age of expansion, when opportunities for profitable investment are never lacking, thriftiness instead of appearing as a cause of unemployment, appears as a cause of investment, and all the increased wealth which results from the accumulation of capital equipment — houses, roads, machinery — is attributed to the beneficent effects of thrift. This view of thriftiness colours much of traditional economic teaching, and some writers, as we saw, have even sought to justify the unequal distribution of incomes because inequality promotes thriftiness.

At the present day, when the problem of unemployment preoccupies our minds, so that even when a boom begins to develop talk immediately turns to what will happen in the next slump, such a view of thriftiness appears paradoxical, or even pernicious. But in other circumstances thriftiness becomes a social virtue. In war-time, when all resources released from private consumption are immediately snapped up by the military machine, in Soviet Russia, where there is an insatiable demand for new capital equipment, even, to a milder extent, in the age when railway building was absorbing huge amounts of new capital, the choice, for the community, between present consumption and future wealth (or the demands of war) is a real one, and every man who is kept occupied in providing for present consumption is prevented from contributing to new investment, or to the necessities of war.

These examples point the contrast between an ideal system in which abstinence creates real wealth, and the system that we know, in which economy leads to waste and sound finance is the cause of bankruptcy. But they also serve to warn us against too extreme a reaction from the traditional view of thriftiness as the first of the economic virtues.

CHAPTER VI

SUPPOSED REMEDIES FOR UNEMPLOYMENT

CHANGES IN WAGES

WE have seen that employment may be increased by an increase in investment or by a decline in thriftiness. These two categories divide the whole field, and (apart from reductions in efficiency which mean that more labour is required for a given output) any influence that tends to increase employment can be analysed into either an increase in investment or a reduction in thriftiness.

It is sometimes argued that another way to increase employment is to raise wages. If entrepreneurs agree to pay their workers higher rates, money demand for goods is increased, and it is argued from this that activity and output will increase. But this rise in demand merely offsets the rise in cost of production due to higher wages. A larger expenditure of money is now needed to buy the same goods, and the increase in money income is not an increase in real purchasing power. There is no simple remedy for unemployment to be found merely in raising wages.

The reverse argument is also common. It is said that if wages were reduced costs would fall, and therefore entrepreneurs would find it profitable to produce more goods. But money incomes fall as much as costs, and money demand is reduced correspondingly. Any one entrepreneur, by cutting the wage rate which he pays, can increase his profits, but at the same time he is reducing the receipts of other entrepreneurs, and if they all cut wages together none of them is any better off. Any one man in the crowd can get a better view of the procession by standing on a chair, but if they all get up on chairs no one's view is improved.

Any change in money wages will set up a number of complicated repercussions, which may lead to a change in employment, in one direction or the other, to some extent, but (apart from reactions upon the rate of interest, which we shall discuss later) a change in money wages is not likely to lead to any great change in employment in either direction.

MONOPOLY

In times of severe depression restriction schemes are widely adopted in order to keep up prices in particular industries and prevent the profits from disappearing altogether. A violent fall in demand puts entrepreneurs in a desperate position, and any group which can get together and agree to cut down their output by collective action can mitigate their own share in the general disaster. By keeping up the price of their own product, and dismissing workers even more extensively than they would have done if competition had continued to prevail, they benefit themselves at the expense of the consumers and the workers. And because they impoverish consumers and workers they damage other entrepreneurs also, by reducing the demand for their commodities. The whole class of entrepreneurs taken together can do themselves little good by these methods, but any one group can benefit itself at the expense of the rest.

Thus it is natural enough that a time of depression should give birth to a litter of quota systems, amalgamations, price-fixing agreements and even schemes for smashing up productive plant and burning stocks of materials. The strange thing is that this growth of monopolistic practices is often advocated as a remedy for unemployment. The argument is made to sound plausible by confusing a symptom with a cause of disease. When depression sets in profits decline ; therefore, it is said, anything which helps to raise profits will help to remove the depression. And we are asked to believe that dismissing workers and closing down plants is a method of increasing employment. To pursue the argument through all its bewildering paradoxes, and to sort out the few grains of truth that are to be found amongst the chaff of special pleading, would take us too far from the main course of our inquiry, and we must be content to dismiss the matter with the common-sense reflection that scarcity of economic goods (whether natural or artificial) can be a benefit to one section of the community only at the expense of others, and that a net increase of prosperity for the community as a whole cannot arise from the restriction of activity and destruction of resources.

MOBILITY OF LABOUR

It is usual to attribute a large amount of unemployment to " frictions " which prevent workers from moving readily from one occupation or locality to another, and remedies for unemployment are sought in training schemes, in providing facilities for transfer and so forth. Such schemes constitute a remedy for unemployment when activity is at a high level. They serve to reduce the minimum of unemployment which remains even in the best of times. But when unemployment is severe they can be of little use. Lack of mobility of labour can be called a cause of unemployment only when there are unfilled vacancies in some places and idle men in others. When every industry and every locality has its own fringe of unemployed workers there is little to be gained (unless it is desired to even things up between the worst and the least bad districts) by shifting men from place to place.

Lack of mobility is itself largely the result of a high level of unemployment. The individual worker lacks incentive to move to a new locality or learn a new trade when there is no locality and no trade in which he can be certain of finding work. Schemes to promote mobility are all to the good, but there is no remedy for immobility so effective as the development of boom conditions.

Part of unemployment is sometimes ascribed to the " unemployability " of the individuals concerned, but this, like mobility of labour, is largely a matter of degree. Particular workers who are inefficient, unreliable or who have strong political convictions, will suffer more than an average share of unemployment, and when the general level of activity is low they are labelled as " unemployables ". But when a revival of trade sets in the employers' standards of efficiency and docility are perforce relaxed, and in the very height of a boom they are often glad to engage whomever they can get. Thus " unemployability ", like immobility, melts away when the demand for labour is sufficiently strong.

REDUCING THE SUPPLY OF LABOUR

There is a certain class of remedies for unemployment which does not involve an increase in trade activity. Workers may be removed from the labour market by, for instance, raising the school-leaving age, or forbidding married women to take jobs. But this is merely to remove some persons from the category of workers and so to

43

reduce unemployment without increasing employment. Or hours of work may be reduced. This has the effect of spreading a given amount of work round amongst more individuals. It is not properly to be regarded as an increase in employment, though it increases the number of individuals employed, for it has no tendency to increase the amount of work done. These various policies may be regarded as methods of reducing the ill effects of unemployment, and they may be desirable on their own merits, but they provide no remedy for the waste of potential real income and wealth which results from under-employment of productive resources.

CHAPTER VII

PRICES

CHANGES IN PRICES

WE have so far discussed influences which affect the level of output. We must now consider the level of prices. Changes in the general level of prices can come about as a result of three distinct groups of causes. First, a change in prices accompanies a change of activity. At any moment there is a certain amount of productive equipment in existence — factories, farms, plantations, machines, ships, rolling-stock and so forth — and output is increased, when demand expands, by employing more labour with the same equipment. In many lines of production, though not necessarily in all, output per man falls off as a greater rate of output is squeezed from the same equipment. And if the same wage is paid per man, cost per unit of output rises when output per man falls. Therefore it would not pay entrepreneurs to produce a greater rate of output unless prices rose, and a rise in the general level of prices normally accompanies an increase in activity.

Secondly, a change in money wages alters the level of prices corresponding to a given level of activity. In any actual situation a change in money wages is likely to be the consequence of a change in activity, and it may, in its turn, be a cause of changes in investment (particularly, as we shall find, through changes in the rate of interest) or in thriftiness, thus leading to a change in activity. Moreover, an exactly equal all-round change in wages is never seen, and many complications arise from changes in the relative wages of different industries.

But it can be seen that an equal change in all wages which is not accompanied by a change in activity must lead to an equal proportional change in prices.

The raw materials and the capital goods used by one industry are the product of another industry, and, for industry as a whole in the world as a whole, costs of production (apart from changes in the rate of interest) depend upon wages. Let us suppose that there is an all-round rise of money-wage rates of, say, 10 per cent. Then the costs of a given output are raised 10 per cent. ; and (unless something has happened to alter output) prices must rise by 10 per cent. Since receipts and costs are raised in the same proportion, profits are also raised in that proportion. But, as prices have also risen in the same proportion, neither real wages nor real profits are changed.

A rise in wages is demanded by workers in the hope of improving their standard of life, and granted with reluctance by employers, who fear a decline in their profits. But where there is an all-round change the one party is unpleasantly, and the other pleasantly, surprised by the result. Experience, all the same, can never teach that the struggle is vain, for wage bargains are made by particular groups of workers and of employers, and any one group which falls behind when a general movement takes place suffers a loss or gains an advantage at the expense of the rest.

A third type of change in prices comes about from a change in efficiency. As time goes by, capital equipment accumulates and improvements in technique are introduced, so that output per man increases, and if money wages are constant there is a tendency for the price level corresponding to a given level of output to fall. Over a period of generations, the general level of prices will move up or down according as money wages rise by more or by less than efficiency increases.

PRICES AND THE STATE OF TRADE

It is well known that a rise in prices normally accompanies an improvement in trade. We can now see how this comes about. An increase in activity sets on foot a rise in prices of the first type, while the consequent decline in unemployment is likely to lead to a rise of the second type, that is to say, a rise in money wages.

The level of money wages alters with the push and pull of bargaining between employers and workers. Bargaining strength depends upon all sorts of considerations, and varies very much from country to country and from generation to generation. For instance, there was a marked growth in the strength of Trade Union organisation in this country in the latter part of the nineteenth century. But whatever the general situation may be, as between workers and employers, the scales tip in favour of the workers when trade is active and unemployment low, and in favour of the employers when unemployment is severe. Thus an upward movement of wages sets in in good times and a fall in bad times.

The public have become so much accustomed to thinking of the rise in prices that occurs when trade improves that it is commonly said that " rising prices are good for trade ". But this is a very confusing way of looking at the matter. The rise in prices which occurs in the first instance, because demand has increased, is a symptom, not a cause, of the increase in demand. Trade is not stimulated because prices rise, but prices rise because trade is stimulated.

47

The rise in prices does not measure the improvement in trade. If supply is very elastic, because, maybe, there is so much surplus plant, before the revival begins, that output per man falls very little as employment increases, then a large increase in output is accompanied by a very small rise in prices, and the fact that prices have not much risen is all to the good. In the early stages of a revival of trade after a slump prices normally rise very little, and only when unemployment has fallen considerably, and factories are working near to capacity, does a sharp rise in prices set in.

The secondary rise in prices, due to the rise in money wages which comes about when a fall in unemployment strengthens the bargaining position of workers, is not a symptom of improved trade, but an indirect consequence of it, and as we shall find at a later stage in the argument, the revival is more likely to continue if prices do *not* rise for this reason than if they do.

Similarly, a fall in prices may be due to a falling off in demand, or it may be the result of wage-cuts, or it may be due to the accumulation of capital equipment and to improved methods of production. In the first case the fall is a symptom of bad trade, but not a cause of it. In the second case the fall in prices is an indirect consequence of bad trade, since wages fall when unemployment is rife ; and in the last case the fall in prices is a symptom of improved efficiency.

REAL WAGES

A second well-known phenomenon is that real wages, that is, the goods which a man can buy with his wage, fall off as trade improves. Wages, it is said, fail to catch up on prices : when the cost of living rises, as the result of an improvement in trade, money wages do not rise fast enough to offset the rise in prices, and the real-wage rate falls. We are now able to see why this must be so. The initial increase in demand raises prices relatively to money wages, while any rise in wages produces an equivalent further rise in prices ; and prices move ahead of wages as the horizon moves ahead of the traveller.

Any one group of workers whose wages rise faster than the rest gain an advantage, for their money incomes rise faster than the prices of commodities produced by other people. But the price of the commodity which they produce rises faster than the money incomes of other workers, and for all workers taken together the real-wage rate falls as activity increases.

THE RATE OF INTEREST AND PRICES

Another well-known phenomenon is the relationship between changes in Bank rate and changes in prices. The practical experience of banking authorities has taught them that if they desire to bring about a fall in prices (as they may be obliged to do for reasons connected with the foreign exchanges, which we will discuss later), their best course is to engineer a rise in the rate of interest. We can now see how it comes about that this policy is successful. Schemes of investment, as we have seen, are made in the light of a comparison between prospective profits and the rate of interest, and when the rate of interest rises schemes of investment which were profitable at the lower rate of interest cease to be profitable. The rate of production of houses, ships, machinery and so forth, begins to fall off soon after the rise in the rate of interest has made itself felt. Men are thrown out of work, the Multiplier comes into play, the ball of activity rolls downhill, and output

and incomes in all industries decline. And with the lower
level of activity prices are lower.

This is the first stage of the effect of a rise in the rate
of interest, and it is a painful one. As time goes by
new wage-bargains are made and, with the higher level
of unemployment, workers (perhaps after unsuccessful
strikes) are compelled to accept lower money wages. A
fall in money wages is the second stage in the operation of
a rise in the rate of interest. If the fall in prices due to the
fall in wages is sufficient to satisfy the authorities, the rate
of interest can now be lowered again and activity can be
allowed to recover.

When Trade Unions are strong, wages may be prevented from falling, and the system may drag painfully
on for years on end at the first stage in the operation of
Bank-rate policy. And even if wages fall, the fall will
normally be uneven as between trades, those workers who
can least afford a cut being forced, because of the weakness of their position, to take the greatest cuts. Thus the
policy of forcing down prices, even if it is successful in the
end, leads to much loss and suffering and social injustice.

GAINS AND LOSSES FROM CHANGING PRICES

We are now able to see the effects of changing activity
and changing prices upon various classes of the community. At first sight we might be inclined to say that
everyone is pleased when trade improves, but actually this
is not the case. An increase in activity leads to a rise in
prices, an increase in employment, a fall in real-wage rates
and a rise in profits. Workers who were formerly unemployed are now better off, but those who were employed
already suffer from the fall in real wages. Many will gain
from an increased sense of security, but a man who was in

no danger of losing his job in the slump is better off during the slump than when revival sets in. Thus even for the workers a revival in trade is not an unambiguous benefit.

But the chief sufferers from a revival are the fixed-income classes. A large number of contracts, such as salaries and interest on debentures and government loans, are fixed in terms of money. Anyone whose income is fixed in terms of money is better off under slump conditions, provided that the slump is not so severe as to drive debtors to default. The only people who have no cause to complain of a revival of trade are entrepreneurs, whose total receipts rise while a large part of their costs are fixed in terms of money.

A rise in money wages, which, as we have seen, is neutral from the point of view of workers taken as a whole, imposes a further loss of real income upon the fixed-income class, while entrepreneurs gain what their creditors lose. If the receipts of a firm rise, and its debenture interest remains the same, the profits of the ordinary shareholders rise in a greater proportion than total receipts, and since total receipts rise in proportion to prices, real profits are increased.

To sum up : A rise in prices which is a symptom of improving trade is partly beneficial and partly harmful to the workers, since it is accompanied by both an increase in employment and a fall in real wages. A rise in prices which is due to a rise in money wages is, in itself, neutral from the point of view of workers. While a rise in prices, of either kind, is beneficial to entrepreneurs and harmful to the fixed-income class. Since a rise in activity not only leads directly to a rise in prices but is also likely to set a rise in money wages on foot, all those whose income is fixed in terms of money have good reason to dread a prosperous state of trade.

CHAPTER VIII

THE RATE OF INTEREST

THE NATURE OF INTEREST

WE have seen that the rate of interest has an extremely important influence on the level of employment, since it affects the decisions of entrepreneurs as to how much it is worth their while to invest in new capital goods. We must now discuss what it is that determines the rate of interest.

Interest is the payment made for borrowing, that is, for acquiring the use of money for a certain time. The essence of a transaction involving interest is that one man parts with money in return for an I O U from another man. The lender acquires a piece of paper representing his right to repayment, and the borrower acquires the immediate use of the money. The borrower must make some payment to the lender, over and above the eventual repayment of the sum borrowed, for if he did not do so the lender (apart from philanthropy) would have no motive for parting with control over his money, and for undergoing the risk that the borrower (through villainy or mere bad luck) may default when repayment is due. This extra payment is the interest on the loan. The motive of the borrower is that he can use the money to acquire capital goods which he expects to earn at least as much as the interest which he has to pay (or, in the case of private borrowing, because he needs money now more than he expects to need it in the future). The motive of the lender is to receive interest. All transactions involving interest, whether it takes the form of an agreed sum or a share in profits, can be reduced to terms of this simple pattern.

The I O U's (bonds, shares, etc.) can change hands, and the ruling rate of interest is shown in the relationship between the income yielded by a security and the price at which it sells. Thus a fall in security prices means a rise in the rate of interest, and a rise in security prices a fall in the rate of interest.

Suppose that a government loan is issued on the terms: £3 per year for every £100 subscribed to the loan. Then if the bond representing £100 originally subscribed stands at par, this means that the rate of interest is 3 per cent. If it stands at £150, the rate of interest is 2 per cent., and if it stands at £80 the rate of interest is 3¾ per cent.

A share which is expected to earn a dividend of £3 will normally sell for less than £100 when the government bond sells for £100, for the return on the government bond is more certain. No one has any motive for holding a more risky security unless it gives a higher yield than a safer security. In what follows, however, we shall not discuss all the complications involved in the relative yields of different types of securities and we shall speak of *the* rate of interest, meaning the whole complex of interest rates on securities of all sorts.

THE DEMAND FOR MONEY

Anyone who owns money could earn interest, if he chose to lend it. The question therefore arises, Why does anyone hold money at all? This question at first sight seems strange. We would all like to have some more money. But what we would like to have is a larger income, or more wealth. The question now before us does not concern a man's rate of income, reckoned in money terms, or the total wealth which he has acquired by past saving or by inheritance ; it concerns the form in which he holds wealth that he owns. Why should anyone hold part of his wealth in cash or on a current account at his bank, so that it earns no interest, or on deposit account where it earns very low interest, when he might acquire more interest by lending it ?

One reason for holding money arises more or less automatically from the manner in which payments are customarily made. Most people receive their incomes at certain intervals and make payments continuously day by day. Shopkeepers and bus companies, on the other hand, receive payments day by day and make payments at longer intervals. At any moment sums are held in the form of money which the individual owner will shortly be going to pay away to someone else, and it would not be worth while to lend them at interest for the short time before they are to be drawn upon.

The amount of money required for this sort of reason will depend partly upon the intervals at which income is received. Suppose a man has an income of £365 a year, of which he spends the whole on current consumption at a steady rate of £1 per day. If his income is paid weekly, he holds, on average, at least £3 : 10s. in cash (£7 on the first day of each week, and nothing on the last). If his income is paid quarterly he holds, on average, at least £45 : 10s., and if it is paid yearly, £182 : 10s. Thus the amount of money which people require for convenience balances varies with the manner in which their income is received. Given the complex of habits governing the intervals of payments, the demand for convenience balances will depend upon the level of income. If money incomes in general are higher there will be an automatic increase in the amount of money that people want to hold. This fact, as we shall find, is of considerable importance.

Money may also be held by individuals who own a small amount of wealth which they do not feel it worth while to put out at interest. Suppose that the man who is spending the whole of his weekly income of £7 also owns £5, which he has saved in the past, and is keeping as a reserve. Then his average holding of money is £8 : 10s. Again, individuals who have a larger amount of wealth may like to hold a certain sum in readily accessible form, say, in a bank account, as a safeguard against a sudden emergency. A large number of small sums held in the form of money for such reasons as these amount to a considerable total for the community as a whole.

Larger sums may be held by individual owners of wealth who are refraining from buying interest-bearing securities at the moment because they expect them to be cheaper in a short time, that is to say, they are expecting a rise in the rate of interest to take place. If *all* owners of wealth were confidently expecting a rise in the rate of interest, all would be anxious to sell securities at existing prices, and the prices of securities would fall immediately to the point at which no further fall was expected, so that no one would want to hold money. But so long as there are differences of opinion amongst owners of wealth some will be holding money, expecting a future fall in the price of securities, while others are refraining from selling the securities they hold in the expectation that the price is not going to fall. Moreover, no one is ever quite confident that his best guess at what is likely to happen is really a good guess, and many people hold part of their wealth in the form of money just because it is the one thing whose price in terms of money they can be sure will not alter.

THE DEMAND FOR MONEY AND THE RATE OF INTEREST

For these reasons there is always a certain amount of money that people want to hold, in spite of the fact that they can get interest by parting with it. But the higher the rate of interest, other things equal, the less money will they want to hold, for interest represents the sacrifice entailed by holding money. The convenience and the sense of security obtained by owning money are weighed against the interest obtained by parting with it, and the greater the advantage of parting with money the less will people want to hold.

By the amount of money we mean the amount of coins, notes and bank deposits. Individuals possess, at any moment, some coins and notes, or have deposits standing in their names. The sum of all the amounts that they own is the total quantity of money. Deposits which are being held at any moment as convenience balances to bridge the gap between receipts and payments are known as the *active* deposits, because they pass rapidly from one individual to another as payments are made. Deposits which are used as a form of holding accumulated wealth, as an alternative to securities, are *inactive*. In normal times notes and coins belong almost entirely to the active circulation, though perhaps there are still some people who like to keep part of their wealth in the chimney corner. In general, the amount of active deposits which people desire to hold is not much affected by the rate of interest, though a very high rate may tempt people to economise in their convenience balances to some extent. The main influence of the rate of interest upon the amount of money which people want to hold is on the amount of inactive balances.

On any day in the year there is a certain amount of money (notes, coin and bank deposits) in existence, and all this money must be owned by someone. From moment to moment the rate of interest must find its level at the point at which people, taken together, are willing to hold just the amount of money that there is. For if the rate of interest were higher than this level some owners of money would be anxious to buy securities with their money in order to obtain interest. The desire to buy securities drives up their price and so lowers the rate of interest, and this process must be carried to the point at which no owner of money any longer wishes to buy securities. Similarly, if on any day the rate of interest were lower than the level at which people are content to hold the amount of money there is on that day, they would be anxious to sell securities and the rate would rise. Thus, given the total of wealth in existence, the ruling level of income, and the state of expectations about the future, the rate of interest is determined from moment to moment by the quantity of money. Just now, as you read this page (unless it is out of office hours), to-day's rate of interest is being determined, and is moving to the level at which no one who owns securities wants to sell them and no one who owns money wants to buy them.

THE SUPPLY OF MONEY

The quantity of money, in turn, is determined by the banking system, acting within the framework of certain legal and customary rules. The most important part of the supply of money, in modern conditions, is represented by bank deposits, and it is through the action of the banks that the amount of money is controlled.

In the British system the banks keep a certain ratio

(about 1 to 9) of " cash " to other assets. " Cash " consists of notes and coins in the tills of the banks and deposits with the Bank of England, which are regarded as equivalent to actual cash. The other assets of the banks consist of bills, advances and securities. These all represent loans of different kinds, and since there is no difference of principle between one and another we may conveniently lump them all together under the title of securities. Securities earn interest and cash earns none. The banks therefore do not want to hold an unnecessarily large amount of cash. On the other hand they do not want their ratio of cash to fall below what is traditionally regarded as the safe and respectable figure.

The custom of preserving a strict cash ratio gives the Bank of England power to control the total amount of bank deposits. Let us see how this comes about. When the Bank wishes to increase the amount of deposits, so that the rate of interest may be forced down, it buys securities on the open market. Suppose that a Mr. Snooks parts with £100 worth of gilt-edged securities and receives £100 from the Bank. He pays this £100 into his own bank account. His bank now finds itself with its total of deposits increased by £100 and its assets increased by £100 of cash in its deposit with the Bank of England. To prevent its cash ratio from rising unnecessarily high it makes use of £90 from this £100 to buy securities, thus restoring the ratio of cash to other assets to the customary figure of 1 to 9. But the £90 which it expends in this way now appears as additional deposits and additional cash in the accounts of other banks (a part may come back to the same bank), who consequently buy securities to the extent of £81. And so on round and round until the Bank's original purchase of £100 of securities from Mr. Snooks has led to an increase in the total of deposits of £1000, against which the banks hold £100 more cash and £900 more securities. The public are now holding £1000 more deposits than before and the banks (including the Bank of England) are holding £1000 more of securities. Thus for every £100 of securities bought by the Bank of England £1000 are bought by the banking system as a whole.

The purchase of securities by the banks drives up their price (thus lowering the rate of interest) to whatever point is required to make the public willing to part with the securities and hold deposits instead. Thus the power to induce an increase in the total amount of bank deposits enables the Bank of England to bring about a fall in the rate of interest when it wishes to do so. The reverse process, of selling securities in the open market and forcing the banks to reduce deposits, is used when a rise in the rate of interest is required. Control by these " open market operations " is supplemented by the direct control of Bank rate, which is kept in step with the movements of the general complex of interest rates dictated by the Bank's policy.

The freedom of action of the Bank is not absolute, for when the gold standard is in force it is obliged to regulate its operations in such a way as to maintain an adequate gold reserve, and even when there is no gold standard it is still obliged to consider the stability of the foreign exchanges. This matter will be considered in a later chapter.

In most other banking systems the control of the Central Bank is not so well established as in the British system, but in all countries the same principles are at work, though they may show themselves in somewhat different forms. In every case the banking system as a whole determines the amount of deposits, and lowers or raises the rate of interest by buying or selling securities and increasing or reducing the amount of deposits held by the public.

Thus, within the limits set by its legal or customary obligations, the banking system can control the rate of interest by operating on the quantity of money.

Normally the banks operate directly only upon the short-term rate of interest, but if the yield on one kind of security falls, people sell out that kind of security in order to buy others, and so the rise in price and fall in yield is transmitted to all classes of securities until the whole complex of interest rates is affected.

Changes in the Demand for Money

If the banking authorities wish to keep the rate of interest constant, they must offset changes in the demand for money by altering the quantity of money. First, the gradual increase in the total of wealth which comes about as investment continues year after year will increase the amount of money which people require to hold. Thus the quantity of money must gradually increase as time goes by if the rate of interest is to be prevented from rising.

Second, a change in trade activity alters the demand for money. When trade is more active and employment greater, the amount of money which people require for the active circulation goes up. Similarly, a rise in money wages and prices raises the demand for money. Thus when trade improves or wages rise the rate of interest will rise unless the quantity of money is increased.

Finally, a change in the state of confidence about the future alters the amount of wealth which the owners of wealth want to hold in the form of money, at a given rate of interest, in order to feel a sense of security. Thus, if the demand for money rises as the result of an upset to confidence, the quantity of money must be increased in order to prevent the rate of interest from rising.

It is here that we find the proper significance of " hoarding ". An increase in the desire to hold money, as opposed to securities, will tend to drive up the rate of interest, and so to bring about a fall in activity. But there is no connection between this and the fall in activity directly produced by an increase in the desire to save.

A Change in the Rate of Interest

We are now able to see how the causes and the consequences of a change in the rate of interest react upon each other. Let us suppose that the Bank of England carries out open-market purchases and the other banks respond in the usual way by bringing about an increase in the total of deposits. In the first instance nothing has happened to the total of wealth, the level of incomes, or the state of confidence, but the banks are holding more securities and the public have parted with securities and are holding deposits instead. The rate of interest is therefore forced down to the point at which the public are willing to hold the additional deposits. The rate falls, say, from 4 per cent. to $3\frac{1}{2}$ per cent.

After the rate of interest has ruled at $3\frac{1}{2}$ per cent. for a few months, schemes of investment which were not being undertaken at 4 per cent., but which are profitable at $3\frac{1}{2}$ per cent., begin to be carried out. Men are set to work at building and so forth, activity and incomes increase in accordance with the Multiplier, and an improvement in trade sets in. Now, supposing that no further change in the quantity of money takes place, the rate of interest will rise somewhat, for with larger incomes the requirements of the active circulation are increased. It rises, at this stage, perhaps to $3\frac{3}{4}$ per cent., but it cannot go back to 4 per cent., for if it did investment would relapse to its former level and the increased demand for convenience balances would disappear again.

With increased employment the position of workers is strengthened, and a rise in money wages may set in. With each rise in wages and prices the demand for money for convenience balances is increased, people find it necessary to sell out securities in order to provide themselves with a fund of cash, and the rate of interest is driven up. The higher the level of money wages the greater is the demand for money at a given level of activity, and once wages are up they will not easily come down again, even when employment falls off. Thus the rate of interest may be driven, by the rise in wages, back towards the 4 per cent. at which it originally stood, so that the stimulus to trade activity disappears.

We have here seen one of the most important influences which brings a revival of trade to an end. Normally, for whatever reason a revival may begin, it will lead to a rise in the rate of interest, which checks investment and brings the revival to an end. A revival in trade is always in danger of cutting its own throat.

Moreover, we have now seen why it is that in normal times full employment can never be attained. When unemployment has fallen very low, a rapid rise in money wages sets in, the demand for money in the active circulation increases, the rate of interest is driven up, investment falls off and unemployment increases again.

LIMITS TO THE CONTROL OF THE RATE OF INTEREST

Even if the banking authorities wished to control the rate of interest in such a way as to prevent unemployment they would not find it easy to do so. For the mere accumulation of capital leads to a fall in prospective profits and (unless inventions or increases in population take place sufficiently rapidly) investment is always tending to bring itself to an end. To preserve full employment the rate of interest would have to be constantly falling. A sufficient fall in the actual rate of interest is hard to bring about, first, because no one country can lower its rate of interest very far unless the rest of the world follows suit, secondly, because powerful vested interests are opposed to very low interest rates, and thirdly, because legal and customary rules (particularly when the gold standard is in use) limit the powers of the monetary authorities to control the rate of interest.

Moreover, to preserve full employment the rate of interest would often have to make violent jumps. Prospective profits are much influenced by optimism and pessimism of entrepreneurs, and very violent changes in the rate of interest may be required to influence investment. At the same time changes in the state of confidence react upon the demand for money, so that violent changes in the quantity of money may be required to influence the rate of interest. The problem of maintaining exactly the right rate of interest to preserve full employment is by no means a simple one.

Even if the rate of interest were deliberately controlled with a view to keeping unemployment as low as possible, oscillations in the state of trade would be hard to prevent. But, in the present state of affairs, the rate of interest is not controlled with this end in view. The chief preoccupation of the authorities is to prevent the rapid rise in prices which sets in when unemployment falls very low, and the fear of this evil seems to be far more present to their minds than fear of the evils of unemployment. As things work out the chief function of the rate of interest is to prevent full employment from ever being attained.

CHAPTER IX

ASPECTS OF THE RATE OF INTEREST

The Earnings of Capital

THE rate of interest is sometimes regarded as being the same thing as the profitability of capital. This is highly misleading. The prospective earnings of capital goods are determined by the general state of trade, and the cost of production of capital goods by technical conditions and the level of money wages in the industries that produce them. These two sets of influences determine the profitability of capital. The rate of interest is the price that has to be paid to borrow money. These are two quite different things, determined by quite different causes. There is a tendency for them to be brought to equality with each other, for if profitability is greater than the rate of interest, entrepreneurs have a motive to create more capital goods, and as the amount in existence increases, their earnings per unit fall. To return to our first example, if a house bringing in a net income of £50 a year costs £1000 to build, and the rate of interest is 4 per cent., then houses of this type will continue to be built until they are so plentiful that the rents at which they can be let yield a net income of only £40.

A rise in the profitability of capital goods with the same rate of interest, or a fall in the rate of interest with the same profitability, will lead to an increase in the number of capital goods in existence sufficient to restore the rate of profit to equality with the rate of interest. The rate of profit and the rate of interest are not the same thing, and they tend to be equal simply because, when they differ, it pays entrepreneurs to act in such a way as to bring the rate of profit into equality with the rate of interest.

THE REWARD OF WAITING

The rate of interest is also sometimes regarded as the "reward of waiting". This is an ambiguous phrase. It is often used to mean the reward for saving. But this view does not hold water. It is true that the ruling rate of interest may have an effect upon the amount that individuals want to save, but any owner of wealth can get interest by lending it, no matter whether he is at present adding to his wealth by saving or not. Thus interest as a reward for saving is not at all on a par with wages as a reward for work. No one can earn wages this week without working this week, but a man whose ancestors saved (or, for that matter, committed highway robberies) a hundred years ago can receive interest without doing any saving at all.

This objection does not arise if we interpret "waiting" to mean merely spending less on current consumption than the total purchasing power at command. On this view interest is the reward for not bluing your capital. There is a certain moral flavour about the idea of a "reward for waiting", as something comparable with the reward for working, which wears very thin when it is interpreted to mean merely a reward for owning wealth.

But the rate of interest is not even a reward for owning wealth, for a man may own wealth and hold it in the form of money, which earns no interest. We return therefore to our starting-point — the rate of interest is simply the payment for lending money.

The Regulator

Finally, the rate of interest is regarded as a regulator of the economic system. On this view the rate of interest is determined by the supply and demand of new capital, so that, when people become more thrifty, it is held that the rate of interest falls in such a way as to promote a corresponding increase in investment in new capital goods, while, if the profitability of capital goods is increased, it is held that the rate of interest is driven up in such a way as to limit the increase in investment to whatever increase in the desire to save may be induced by the higher rate of interest.

This theory is untenable. It is true, indeed, that an increase in the desire to save tends to lower the rate of interest, but it only does so because it reduces activity and so brings about a fall in the demand for money. And it is true that an increase in investment normally raises the rate of interest, by increasing activity and so raising the demand for money. But whatever the rate of investment may be, incomes will always be such that people save at whatever rate provides the capital which entrepreneurs are investing. A change in demand for capital (investment) always brings about (by way of a change in incomes) an exactly equal change in supply (saving); while if willingness to supply capital (thriftiness) increases, but the demand for it (investment) does not go up, no more will actually be saved than before. Thus it is clearly absurd to say that the rate of interest is determined by the supply and demand of capital.

Nevertheless the conception of the rate of interest as the regulator of the economic system contains an important element of truth. We are concerned nowadays with the problem of unemployment, and the paradox of poverty in the midst of plenty overshadows all discussions of economic questions. The failure of a system of private enterprise to regulate itself in such a way as to prevent the waste and misery of unemployment appears to us, in the present age, as its most striking feature. But within very broad limits the system does regulate itself. Very severe unemployment does, slowly and imperfectly, bring about its own cure. For when unemployment is severe then, on the one hand, money wages are driven down, so that the demand for money is reduced, while, on the other hand, the authorities are under pressure to increase the quantity of money in order to help things out. Thus, in a broad general sense, it is true that unemployment causes the rate of interest to fall. At the same time, a very high level of employment leads to a rise in the rate of interest. For as the limit of full employment is approached money wages rise rapidly, and the authorities are anxious to prevent a corresponding increase in the supply of money, so that the rate of interest is forced up.

Thus, when unemployment rises very high or falls very low, counteracting influences are called into play, and the fluctuations of employment are held within certain limits. For the discussion of problems involving broad changes over the course of generations, in population, the rate of technical progress or the general social forces influencing thriftiness, it is possible to regard fluctuations in employment as a secondary consideration, and to conduct the discussion in terms of a self-regulating system. Then, taking a short cut, we may speak as though an increase in the profitability of capital were the cause of a rise in the rate of interest, and an increase in thriftiness the cause of a fall.

We have seen already that, when the motive for investment is strong, an increase in thriftiness may be regarded as a cause of an increase in investment. We now see that there is a more general sense in which thriftiness may be said to cause investment. For when the level of employment is fixed an increase in thriftiness must lead (by way of lowering the rate of interest) to an increase in investment. And in so far as it is true that in reality employment can move only between certain limits it is true that a large-scale increase in thriftiness must lead to a more or less commensurate increase in investment.

A large part of economic theory has been devoted to the study of an ideal self-regulating system, and it is important not to lose sight, in our preoccupation with unemployment, of the principles derived from such a system, which apply in a broad general way to the actual world.

CHAPTER X

CHANGES IN THE SUPPLY OF MONEY

GOLD-MINING

WE have seen how the creation of additional bank deposits can come about at the initiative of the Central Bank. This operation has no direct effect upon income, for the mere fact that the banks are holding more securities and the public are holding more deposits has no immediate reaction upon anyone's income. At the same time, it has an effect upon income in a roundabout way, because it leads to a fall in the rate of interest, and consequently to an increase in the rate of investment in capital goods.

There are, however, two ways in which the supply of money may be increased which have a direct effect upon the level of incomes, as well as an indirect effect *via* the rate of interest. The first way is by gold-mining. People who make their incomes, whether wages or profits, from gold-mining are in a somewhat similar position to those engaged upon erecting the Tower of Babel. Their activity adds neither to the current output of consumption goods nor to the useful capital equipment of industry. But the expenditure which they make from their incomes is laid out upon consumption goods, and the demand for consumption goods increases when increased incomes are made from gold-mining. Thus gold-mining is on a par with investment in capital goods, as far as its effect upon employment, profits and prices is concerned, while it is going on, though what it leaves behind as a permanent addition to the stock of wealth is not directly useful, like houses or machines, but has only a conventional value.

The increase in the stock of gold above the surface of the earth, which results from mining, has a further effect upon the situation, for it leads to an increase in the stock of money. Wherever the gold standard is in operation Central Banks are obliged to buy gold as it is presented to them, and a purchase of gold by a Central Bank has precisely the same effects as a purchase of securities in the open market. The seller of the gold deposits the sum he receives for it at his own bank ; the bank finds its " cash " increased by this sum, and the whole chain of consequences follows the course which we have already traced.

When Central Banks wish to fulfil their obligations under the gold standard but do not wish to be forced into increasing the quantity of money just because gold happens to be offered to them, they can offset the purchase of gold by the sale of a corresponding amount of securities. The total of " cash " for the banks then remains the same, and the only change is that the Central Bank holds gold in place of securities. This is called " sterilising " the gold, since the quantity of money cannot then increase and multiply in the usual way.

These manœuvres, by which gold is dug from the earth in order to be buried in the vaults of a Central Bank, would seem strange and arbitrary to an observer from Mars ; they have developed by a gradual process, within the framework of legal rules devised to meet the needs of an earlier stage of monetary evolution, and are not the product of any rational plan.

CREATION OF MONEY THROUGH A BUDGET DEFICIT

A budget deficit financed by borrowing from the Central Bank has effects similar to those of gold-mining.

We have already seen how a budget deficit influences incomes. If there is an increase in government expenditure without any corresponding increase in tax receipts there will be an increase in incomes and activity. This is true equally whether the government borrows from the public or from the Central Bank. If the borrowing is from the public there is no further effect to be considered. But if borrowing is from the Central Bank, then on top of the direct effect of the deficit upon income there is the effect of an increase in the quantity of money. For the Central Bank, in lending to the government, increases the " cash " of the banks, just as it does by buying securities or by buying gold. The direct effect of the deficit comes to an end as soon as the budget is balanced, but the effect upon the quantity of money remains as a permanent legacy.

The increase in the quantity of money, which takes place cumulatively as long as the deficit is running, will tend to produce a fall in the rate of interest and (unless confidence has been badly shaken) the effects of an increase in investment, induced by lower interest rates, will be superimposed upon the direct effects of the budget deficit in increasing consumption.

At first there will be a drag upon the fall in the rate of interest because the direct effect of the budget deficit in increasing incomes raises the demand for money, since the requirements of the active circulation depend upon the level of income. But the increase in demand for money will be very slight (so long as money wages do not rise) compared to the increase in supply, and it is a once-and-for-all effect, while the increase in the supply of money is cumulative.

Suppose, for instance, that the Multiplier is 3, and that the active circulation increases by £1 million for every £4 million a year of income. Then a budget deficit at the rate of, say, £12 million a year will lead to an increase in income of £36 million a year (because the Multiplier is 3) and consequently to an increase in the active circulation of £9 million. But the loans of the Central Bank to the government are increasing " cash " at the rate of £1 million a month, so that, if the banks maintain a ratio of cash to other assets of 1 to 9, one month's deficit will lead to an increase of deposits of £10 million, and already before a month has elapsed enough new money will have been created to meet the increase of £9 million in the active circulation. In the early part of the month there is a tendency for the rate of interest to rise, but this tendency is quickly overcome and reversed as the increase in the quantity of money accumulates.

The whole difference between a budget deficit financed by creating money and one financed by ordinary borrowing lies in this reaction upon the rate of interest.

In our numerical example we have taken money wages as constant. A rise in wages enhances the increase in the demand for money due to increased activity, and if unemployment falls so low, under the influence of the deficit, that a rapid rise in money wages sets in, the demand for money may increase to any extent, and may rush ahead of the increase in supply, so that the rate of interest is pushed sharply upward. This situation — a budget deficit financed by borrowing from the Central Bank, unemployment tending to disappear, money wages rising rapidly, an increasing supply of money lagging behind the increase in incomes, and a violent rise in the rate of interest — was characteristic of the later phase of the great German inflation of 1921–3.

Precisely the same consequences follow if the government meets its deficit simply by printing legal-tender notes as if it meets it by borrowing from the Central Bank. For the public is not obliged to hold more notes merely because more have been printed. Notes which the public do not require are deposited in the banks ; the cash of the banks is consequently increased just as it is by an increase in Central Bank assets, and a tendency for the rate of interest to fall is superimposed upon the direct effect of a deficit in increasing activity.

A Social Dividend

In the light of the foregoing analysis we can discuss the proposal to institute a Social Dividend financed by creating money. Under this scheme every citizen would receive a note for, say, £1 by the first post every Saturday, the new notes being printed as required. To conventional minds this scheme sounds altogether too fantastic to be taken seriously, and its advocates have done it some disservice by the exceedingly complicated and unconvincing arguments which they use in support of it. But all the same it recommends itself to common sense. If there is unemployment on the one hand and unsatisfied needs on the other, why should not the two be brought together, by the simple device of providing the needy with purchasing power to consume the products of the unemployed ?

How would such a scheme work out ? In practice (as some tentative experiments in this direction have already shown) it is likely to run upon the rocks through raising opposition from powerful financial interests, but, assuming that it is allowed to work smoothly, it would produce the desired effect of increasing consumption, and therefore employment, in just the same way as an ordinary budget deficit does. The extra pound-a-weeks would be spent, all or in part, upon food and clothes and amusements, trade would prosper, prices rise and unemployment fall. Further, the cumulative increase in the stock of money would bring about a fall in the rate of interest (provided panic was avoided) and so encourage investment, thus giving a further stimulus to activity.

The drawback of the scheme lies in the fact that it robs the monetary authorities of all their power, for while it is in force they can no longer control the quantity of money. When unemployment has been reduced to a minimum and no further increase in real income is possible, a rapid rise in money wages is likely to set in. But still week by week the cumulative increase in the quantity of money would continue, and there would be no defence against the violent rise in prices, collapse of the exchange and general confusion associated with galloping inflation.

Economic life presents us always with a choice of evils, and differences between the orthodox bankers and the currency reformers arise because each chooses a different evil. The bankers are afraid, above everything, of inflation, and are light-hearted in allowing unemployment to occur ; currency enthusiasts, on the other hand, see the evils of unemployment and mock at the dangers of inflation ; while both differ from more radical reformers in hoping to preserve or to patch up the system of private enterprise, rather than to recast it altogether.

APPENDIX

The Quantity Theory of Money

Discussions of prices and trade activity are often conducted in terms of what is known as the " Quantity Theory of Money ". This is a somewhat misleading title, for actually there is nothing in it that can strictly be called a theory. There is, firstly, the view that an increase in the quantity of money is likely to lead to a rise in prices. We have seen why this view is in general correct — an increase in the quantity of money tends to reduce the rate of interest, a fall in the rate of interest promotes investment, an increase in investment leads to a general increase in activity, and an increase in activity is accompanied by a rise in prices — but a vague general statement that an increase in the quantity of money is likely to lead to a rise in prices cannot properly be described as a theory of money. Secondly, there is a method of approaching the problems of prices by means of an equation involving the quantity of money. This is not a theory of money, but a particular method of analysis.

The simplest form of the Quantity Equation is $MV = PT$. M is the quantity of money (coins, notes and bank deposits), P is an index of the general level of prices, and T is an index of the volume of transactions per unit of time. V is the velocity of circulation ; it represents the number of times that a unit of money, on average, is used to make a transaction in the unit of time. If T represents transactions per year, V is the number of times that a unit of money changes hands during a year. If T is reckoned for a week, V is the number of times that a unit of money changes hands in a week ; and so forth. If we reckon by the year, PT (the annual value of transactions) is, say, £50,000 million. Then if M, the quantity of money, is, say, £2000 million, V is equal to 25. If we reckon by the week V is equal to roughly $\frac{1}{2}$, and so forth.

Now it is clearly true that $MV = PT$, for PT is the value of the sum of all transactions made during the period with the aid of money, and MV is the sum of all the units of money used in making those transactions. The two are equal because they are two sides of the same thing. But for that very reason the equation cannot possibly tell us anything that we do not know already. We can see from the equation that if, for instance, something happens to raise T, then either P must fall, or M or V must rise. In fact we know (though the equation itself cannot tell us) that in reality a rise in T, the volume of transactions, is normally accompanied by a rise, not a fall, in prices. We can then proceed with this knowledge to say that if something happens to increase T, PT will increase by more. Now the equation tells us that if PT increases either M or V must increase. PT is determined, roughly speaking, by the level of trade activity, and M is controlled by the banking system. We can therefore proceed to say that if something happens to increase PT, but the banks do not increase M, then V must rise.

The argument of Chapter VIII enables us to see how this comes about. If something happens to increase trade activity the demand for money in the active circulation is increased. If the banks do not increase the total amount of money, the rate of interest rises, and, it being now less worth while to hold wealth in the form of money instead of in securities, inactive deposits are reduced as much as the active deposits have increased. The average velocity of circulation of money is therefore raised. Thus an increase in V is brought about as a consequence of an increase in PT. This is all very well, but we have been telling the equation what is happening, it has not been telling us.

More often the equation is read right-handed, thus : if M is increased, then unless V falls in the same proportion, PT must rise. This sounds more helpful, but in fact it obscures the real point. For, as we have seen, an increase in the quantity of money produces its effect upon trade activity by way of a reduction in the rate of interest. Thus it shows itself in the first instance, before PT has had time to alter, precisely in a fall in V. When the quantity of money is increased by the banks buying securities, the whole increase goes immediately into the inactive deposits, where its velocity is zero, and the average velocity of circulation is reduced in exact proportion to the increase in the quantity of money. It is only after the fall in the rate of interest which accompanies an increase in the inactive circulation has had time to produce its effect upon trade activity, and so upon PT, that the increase in M leads to an increase in MV.

No one who understands the rules of logic ever expected a truism, such as $MV = PT$, to tell us anything that we do not know without it, but in inexpert hands the Quantity Equation can lead to great confusion. There are two main criticisms on the habits of thought which it fosters. First, it leads people to discuss changes of prices without making the vital distinction between a change due to a change on the side of demand, such as the rise in prices which accompanies an increase in investment or a reduction in thriftiness, and a change of prices due to a change on the side of supply, such as the rise in prices which is produced by a rise in money wages. Second, it leads people to attribute some kind of direct influence upon prices to changes in the quantity of money, so that some writers seem to suggest that bank-notes have feet, and run into the shops and bid up prices as soon as they are printed. Changes in the quantity of money are of the utmost importance, but their importance lies in their influence upon the rate of interest, and a theory of money which does not mention the rate of interest is not a theory of money at all.

For detailed discussion of changes in trade activity the Quantity Equation is a weak and treacherous instrument. But when we are concerned with broad problems of the movement of prices over the course of generations, it comes into its own. For, as we have seen, an increase in the quantity of money, by lowering the rate of interest and promoting trade activity, leads to a rise in money wages, and since it is easier to raise wages than to lower them, each burst of activity leaves behind a permanent legacy of raised prices. On the other hand if the quantity of money refuses to increase, when population and the general volume of activity is increasing, then the rate of interest will be kept at a high level, trade will be chronically stagnant, workers will be in a weak position *vis-à-vis* employers, and money wages will be stationary or will even tend to fall. Thus the quantity of money exercises a preponderating influence upon the broad movements of prices over the course of history.

CHAPTER XI

FOREIGN TRADE

FOREIGN INVESTMENT

NATIONAL boundaries have for the most part been ignored in the foregoing argument. We must now examine certain questions from the point of view of a single country. First of all we must consider the balance of trade, that is to say, the surplus of exports over imports (or of imports over exports). The items composing the balance of trade include both " visible " imports and exports, that is, physical goods moved across national boundaries, and " invisible " imports and exports, such as shipping services, interest on loans, and tourist expenditure, involving payments from the nationals of one country to the nationals of another. It represents the balance of payments on income account between one country and the rest of the world, as opposed to the capital account, represented by international lending and borrowing.

Now, from the point of view of one country, an excess of exports over imports has all the characteristics of investment. Incomes earned by selling goods to foreigners, just like incomes earned by making capital goods, add to the demand for home-produced consumption goods without adding to the supply currently available to be consumed, while home-earned income expended upon foreign-produced goods is subtracted from the demand for home-produced goods. Thus an increase in exports or a decrease in imports sets the Multiplier to work, creates secondary employment and brings about an increase in home income and home saving ; in short, produces all the effects upon home activity of an increase in investment.

At the same time, when exports exceed imports the citizens of the rest of the world are, on balance, becoming indebted to the citizens of the home country, for they are consuming more home-produced goods than they are paying for currently. Citizens of the home country are therefore acquiring foreign securities at a rate equal to the excess of exports over imports. Thus the surplus of exports, which represents the *foreign investment* of the home country, adds to the wealth of the home community, and in this respect also it resembles the creation of capital goods.

But from the point of view of the world as a whole the foreign investment of one country is not investment at all. If one country increases its surplus of exports to the rest of the world, the rest of the world must increase its surplus of imports from that country to an equal extent, and there is an increase of unemployment in the rest of the world which offsets the increase of employment in that country. Moreover, as citizens of that country increase their holding of securities representing loans to the rest of the world, the citizens of the rest of the world are increasing their indebtedness to that country, and for the world as a whole there is no increase in wealth.

HOME ACTIVITY AND FOREIGN INVESTMENT

An increase in activity inside one country generally leads to a decline in its foreign investment. For when larger incomes are being earned there is an increase in expenditure, of which part falls upon foreign goods. When house-building increases at home the newly employed labourer buys more American tinned fruit, the foreman can afford petrol for his motor-bicycle and the contractor takes his holiday on the Riviera. The demand for imports is increased, while nothing has happened to cause a corresponding expansion of exports, so that foreign investment falls off as home investment increases. This is merely another way of putting the fact, which we observed earlier, that the Multiplier for one country is less than for the whole world as a whole.

If the reduction of unemployment at home leads to a rise in money wages then foreign investment is still further reduced. Money incomes at home are raised, while the prices of foreign goods are unchanged, so that more of them will be purchased. Further, the rise in home wages raises the price of home-produced goods and gives a competitive advantage to foreign goods. At the same time, costs of export goods are raised so that less can be sold. In short, a rise in money wages in one country causes an increase in imports for that country and a decline in exports, so that its rate of foreign investment falls off.

If any one country goes far ahead of the rest in increasing home investment it loses a large part of the benefit, both of increased employment and of increased wealth, through the decline in foreign investment which an increase in home investment brings about.

The importance of this consideration obviously depends upon the extent to which a particular country is engaged in foreign trade. A small, highly specialised country, which imports a large part of what it consumes and exports a large part of what it produces, suffers a severe loss of foreign investment when home investment increases, while a large, almost self-supporting country is little affected.

Public Works in One Country

We must now modify the statement that public works in slump conditions involve no real cost at all to the community which makes them. This is true for a closed community, but for a single country trading with the rest of the world the loss of foreign investment must be taken into account. Thus, instead of saying that the real cost of public works to the community is nil, because the resources employed would have stood idle if the public works had not been undertaken, we must say that the real cost lies in the foreign investment which would have taken place if the public works had not been made, and does not take place when they are made. It is therefore not the case that public works are worth undertaking from a purely national point of view even if they are of no more use than the Tower of Babel. But so long as they have even a moderate value the case for undertaking them remains strong. Suppose that public works, involving an outlay of £100 million, causes a loss of foreign investment, by reducing exports and increasing imports, of £25 million. Then if the real value of the works to the community is reckoned to be not less than £25 million they are still worth undertaking for their own sake, quite apart from the benefits of increased employment which are enjoyed while they are being carried out.

The Foreign Exchanges

The rate of exchange between currencies is determined by the supply and demand for home currency in terms of foreign currencies. Foreign currency is required by home citizens in order to pay their debts abroad, that is, to pay for imports, or to make loans abroad, while home currency is required by foreigners to pay for exports from the home country or to make loans to the home country. An increase in the surplus of exports over imports leads to an increase in the foreign demand for home currency relatively to the supply, and so tends to raise the exchange rate, while an increase in the desire of home citizens to lend abroad (to purchase foreign securities) increases the demand for foreign currency and tends to lower the exchange rate. The exchange is in equilibrium, tending neither to rise nor to fall, when, at the ruling rate, the surplus of exports over imports is equal to the net amount of foreign lending, or the surplus of imports is equal to the net amount of foreign borrowing, as the case may be.

We have seen that an increase in activity in one country leads to a decline in the surplus of exports. It therefore tends to weaken the exchange rate. If the exchange rate is allowed to fall, home industries are protected and export industries stimulated, for, with a lower exchange rate and the same internal prices at home and abroad, foreign goods are dearer at home and home goods cheaper abroad. The fall in exchange therefore acts as a break upon the decline in foreign investment which takes place when home investment increases, and keeps a larger share of secondary employment within the home country. It might be argued therefore that a fall in the exchange rate is an excellent thing. But there are some circumstances in which it cannot be allowed to occur.

First of all, if the country is committed to the gold standard the monetary authorities are obliged to keep the exchange steady. To adhere to the gold standard means that the monetary authorities offer to buy and sell gold at a fixed price in terms of the home currency. Now, when the exchange rate falls below the parity set by the fixed gold value of the home currency relatively to the gold value of foreign currencies, it becomes profitable to buy gold at the fixed home price and sell it at the fixed foreign price, using the foreign currency so obtained to buy home currency at the depreciated rate, thus making a profit on the round trip. This very fact prevents the exchange rate from falling below the gold parity by more than the narrow margin which is sufficient to cover the expenses of such operations, but at the same time it means that when the exchange rate tends to be weak the monetary authorities are in danger of losing all their gold. And it is necessary for them to maintain a reserve of gold in order to meet their obligation to sell gold to all comers. Therefore it is necessary for them to create conditions in which the exchange rate does not tend to fall.

Even if the strict obligations of the gold standard are not in force the authorities may be reluctant to allow the exchange to fall, from fear of provoking foreign countries to retaliate. Moreover, there is always a danger that too sharp a fall in the exchange rate may lead to complete collapse. For if the initial fall in the exchange rate is taken by speculators as a sign that a further fall is coming, they begin to buy foreign currency, hoping for a profit when it appreciates, and so precipitate a violent fall in the exchange value of the home currency. A mild dose of exchange depreciation, in suitable conditions, may be beneficial to the home country, but a sudden and drastic fall is highly undesirable, and the authorities regard it as their duty to avoid it at all costs. For these reasons, amongst others, the monetary authorities may feel obliged to prevent a fall in the exchange rate from taking place.

The weapon by which the authorities control the foreign exchange is the rate of interest. A rise in the home rate of interest has a triple effect upon the exchanges. First, it inclines foreigners to lend to the home country, and disinclines home citizens to lend abroad. It therefore increases the demand for home currency relatively to the supply, and strengthens the exchange. This reaction is immediate. As time goes by a second influence comes into operation. With a higher rate of interest investment at home falls off, and employment and incomes decline. This, as we have seen, curtails expenditure upon imports along with expenditure on home goods, and so increases the surplus of exports. The exchange is thus strengthened. Finally, but only after the elapse of many wretched years, money wages at home may be driven down by the pressure of unemployment. Export industries are then stimulated and it is possible to permit a higher level of home consumption without imperilling the exchange. The rate of interest, therefore, can be lowered again when a sufficient fall in money wages has taken place. Thus an increase of prosperity at home weakens the exchange rate and the exchange rate can be restored only by killing prosperity.

EXPANSION IN ONE COUNTRY

We can now see how the authorities of any one country are limited in their power to foster a high level of employment at home. Anything which they do to stimulate activity at home leads to trouble with the exchange rate. Public works, redistributional taxation, a budget deficit, all lead, by increasing home consumption, to an increase in imports relatively to exports, a decline in the balance of trade, and consequently a fall in the exchange rate. Thus the national authorities must be cautious in considering how far it is safe to go, and even when they feel a sincere desire to reduce unemployment at home they may have a very limited power to do so.

But the dangers of an expansionist policy are some-times exaggerated, as an excuse for inaction. The country which brings about an increase in activity at home is benefiting the rest of the world, for the very fact that its demand for import goods rises with increased home employment means that activity in other countries is increased. This improvement may lead to a revival of optimism and set home investment on foot in those countries also. The home country will then benefit in its turn from increased activity in the rest of the world. Thus any one important country which takes a bold course may lead the world to prosperity, while if each sits timidly waiting for some other to begin, all must continue in misery.

THE RATE OF INTEREST IN ONE COUNTRY

Each national government is limited in its power to carry out expansionist policies such as public works schemes. A national monetary authority is even more circumscribed in its power to control the home rate of interest. If the rate of interest is lowered in one country the exchange is weakened for two reasons. Not only does the consequent increase in home investment lead to a decline in the balance of trade, but also the relative reduction in home interest rates encourages foreign lending, for a better return can now be obtained abroad than at home. Thus any one national authority which endeavours to foster home activity by reducing the rate of interest is in danger of precipitating a collapse of the exchange rate, and no one is able to go far unless the rest are prepared to follow.

Each one claims excuse for maintaining the rate of interest at a level which causes unemployment in the fact that none is free to act alone. But a cautious spirit in each individually is damaging to all collectively. A high rate of interest in any one country weakens the exchanges of the rest (and attracts gold from them if the gold standard is in force). They are driven to defend their exchange rates (and protect their gold reserves) by raising their own interest rates, and so, the world over, the rate of interest is driven up, investment is discouraged, unemployment increases, and misery spreads from one country to another. A share in the sufferings imposed upon the world by a policy of high interest rates comes home to roost to the country which starts the movement, and too narrow a regard for the national advantage may defeat its own ends. Conversely, any one country which lowers its interest rate is benefiting the world, and the advantages of a bold policy come home to roost as well as the evils of timidity.

ECONOMIC NATIONALISM

Unfortunately the governments of the world at the present time appear more prone to snatch an advantage for their own country at the expense of the rest of the world than to carry out policies which benefit the world as a whole. When a severe slump sets in there is unemployment and loss of income in each country. In each country a clamour is raised to defend home industry against foreign competition, and a variety of schemes are devised to reduce imports and increase exports so as to mitigate the decline in home activity.

Of these schemes a tariff upon imports is the most common. The object of a protective tariff is to deflect demand from foreign to home goods and so to increase profits and employment in home industries. An increase in employment in the protected industries leads in the usual way to secondary employment in home consumption - good industries, and to some extent counteracts the effects of the slump.

A competitive advantage can also be obtained for one country by devaluing its exchange, for, as we have seen, this fosters exports, by making home goods cheaper to foreigners, and protects home industry, by making foreign goods dearer at home. Similarly, an advantage can be gained by cutting wages in the home country. An all-round reduction in wages in one country relatively to the rest of the world increases its exports, by making them cheaper, and curtails its imports, by reducing home incomes and prices of home-produced goods relatively to the prices of goods from the outside world. Thus a fall in the exchange rate (provided it does not go too far), or a reduction in wages, improves the balance of trade and increases employment in the country which carries it out.

For every increase of employment at home there is a corresponding increase of unemployment abroad, where export industries have lost their markets and home industries are exposed to competition from cheap imports. For the rest of the world slump conditions become still more severe. From a purely nationalist point of view this in itself is of no importance — if the unemployed are foreigners they are no concern of ours — but it leads to consequences of which the most hard-bitten nationalist must take account. For other countries, finding themselves in a more wretched plight than ever, will have still stronger motives for protecting themselves, by tariffs, devaluation or wage cuts. Retaliation will begin, and before long all the nations of the world will be playing a frantic game of beggar-my-neighbour. As soon as one snatches an advantage it is grabbed back by another, and each is powerless to stand out when the others have begun, for any one nation which refused to join in the game would rapidly be beggared by its less scrupulous neighbours.

Considered collectively all are worse off than before they began. International trade is choked in an entanglement of tariffs, quotas and embargoes and all the benefits of international division of labour are lost to the world. The advantages of exchange stability are forgone. And competition in forcing down wages leads to the waste and bitterness of strikes, the social injustice of arbitrary changes in relative wage rates, and the enhanced burden of indebtedness which follows from a general fall in all values save those fixed in terms of money. All this leaves an evil legacy behind, and even when a world revival sets in and the nations cease their scramble for international trade, the ill-effects of the beggar-my-neighbour policies remain and cannot quickly be undone.

APPENDIX

The Free Trade Controversy

There is a perennial controversy over the merits of free trade and protection, which has never been resolved because, as so often happens, the contestants are talking at cross purposes. The strong point of the free trade case is that artificial barriers to trade lead to inefficiency of production. There is a presumption that the free play of competition will sort out industries as between the various regions of the world in a more economic manner than the whims of politicians. The very fact that an industry needs to be protected in one country shows that it can be conducted more efficiently elsewhere, and protective policies sacrifice the advantage of division of labour between nations, cause economic resources to be used less productively than they might, and so impoverish the world.

The strong point of the protectionist argument is that when home industry is suffering from foreign competition a duty on imports will lead to an increase in the demand for home products, and so increase activity, employment and profits at home.

Now, there is nothing incompatible in those two arguments. The free trade argument shows that tariffs reduce output per man, and the protectionist argument shows that they increase the number of men employed (in the home country — unemployment abroad does not weigh with protectionists). The relative importance of the two arguments varies with the prevalence of unemployment, and, as we have seen, it is in times of depression that the nations of the world are most inclined to resort to protectionist policies. There must always be differences of opinion as to what is the most desirable policy at any moment, but there is no need for dispute about the principles involved.

Unfortunately some fanatical free-traders, over-anxious to establish what they hold to be a righteous cause, have refused to allow any validity at all to the protectionist case, and go so far as actually to deny that a tariff can increase employment in the country that imposes it. Their argument runs as follows : Exports pay for imports, and if imports are cut down, exports must fall off equally. Thus they appear to deny that foreign investment can take place at all — that there can ever be a surplus of exports. When it is pointed out that a surplus of exports can in fact occur, and that the effect of a tariff is to increase it, they fall back upon a further argument. A surplus of exports entails a corresponding amount of lending from the home country to the rest of the world. An increase in the surplus of exports, by increasing foreign lending, depletes the funds available for home industry, and causes home investment to fall off as much as foreign investment increases.

Thus they overlook the fact that an increase in investment leads to an increase in activity and incomes, and consequently to an increase in saving. The increase in foreign investment itself calls into existence the additional savings required to finance it, and there is no reason why home investment should fall off. Quite the contrary.

The decline in imports due to the tariff strengthens the exchange rate and so creates a situation favourable to a fall in the rate of interest, while the increased prosperity of home industry raises prospective profits on capital at home, so that an increase, rather than a decline, in home investment is likely to set in.

If a very high level of employment obtains in the home country the simple argument that " exports pay for imports " comes into its own, for in that case there are no idle resources to be called into employment in the protected home industries, and home industries can expand, to replace imports, only in so far as export industries contract and release labour for their use. But when unemployment is negligible the protectionist argument is irrelevant. Thus the free-traders' argument is valid only when no argument is needed at all.

It is unfortunate for the cause of free trade that such arguments should have been used in its defence, for the true objection to protectionism — that it fosters the interests of each country at the expense of the rest, and so sets the world by the ears — is only obscured by denying that even one country can obtain an advantage from it.

CHAPTER XII

CHANGES IN EMPLOYMENT

THE TRADE CYCLE

WE have now collected the pieces of our jig-saw puzzle, and we must fit them together to form a picture of the fluctuations in employment to which a system of private enterprise is subject.

At any moment trade is always either improving or relapsing, and in the real world " normal times " never come ; we must therefore make an arbitrary choice as to where to take up our story. The most convenient place to begin is the early stage of a trade revival. The rate of investment begins to rise, and consequently activity in the consumption-good industries increases, to the extent dictated by the size of the Multiplier. As output is increasing investment in working capital takes place, and gives a further fillip to activity. Now, the general state of trade has improved and profits are increasing. The lethargy and despair of the slump period leave the souls of entrepreneurs, and their views of future profits begin to be coloured by the higher level of profits ruling in the present. A further expansion of investment therefore takes place. New equipment is ordered to provide for the higher rate of output and new concerns spring up to take advantage of expanding demand. With the higher level of investment, and consequently of expenditure, profits are again increased, prospects are further improved, new schemes of investment undertaken, and the upward movement feeds on itself.

This process may continue over the course of several years. But all the time the products of investment are accumulating — buildings, equipment, ships, improvements to land, and durable capital goods of all kinds are coming into use, and the competition of each new arrival reduces the level of profits for those already in existence. The expansion of investment slows down.

Now, the tragedy of investment is that (unless stimulants are applied) it can never remain at a constant level. For if the rate of investment one year is the same as the last, then, generally speaking, the level of employment and incomes and therefore the level of demand for goods will be the same in the second year as in the first. But all the time capital is accumulating, and in the second year there is a larger amount of equipment available to meet the same demand for commodities. The rate of profit consequently falls off, future prospects are dimmed by the decline in present receipts, and in the third year new investment appears less attractive to entrepreneurs than in the second.

Once investment begins to decline, the Multiplier is set to work in the downward direction, consumption falls off, unemployment increases, and activity and profits decline. The prospects of future profits degenerate under the influence of their present decline, investment falls still further, and the downward movement feeds on itself.

But just as the tragedy of investment lies in the fact that it makes durable additions to real wealth, so a paradoxical comfort is to be found in the fact that capital goods are not permanently durable. Obsolescence and wear and tear deplete the stock of capital, and when activity has ruled at its lowest level for a year or two the gradual decline in the supply of efficient equipment raises the level of profit for that which remains. Here and there investment in making good deficiencies begins to take place, and with an increase in the rate of investment the whole story begins again.

This is the rhythm of investment, which is the main force governing the cycle of trade activity. Other movements are superimposed upon the underlying rhythm. As we have seen, there is a tendency for thriftiness in the capitalist class to decline as prosperity increases, under the influence of a Stock Exchange boom, so that the upswing of activity is enhanced by an increase in the ratio of consumption to investment just when investment itself is increasing. The reaction of spirits which sets in when prosperity begins to decline, and Stock Exchange prices fall, enhances the downward movement, and so the oscillations of trade are exaggerated in each direction.

Changes in sentiment further exaggerate the violence of trade oscillations. We have so far described the process of improving and declining trade as though it took place gradually and smoothly, and this would be the case if entrepreneurs at each moment judged the future level of profits mainly by the current level of profits. But if they develop a state of mind in which increasing profits lead them to expect a further increase in the future, and declining profits a further decline, then the oscillations of investment will be exaggerated, and the turning point will come with greater violence. As soon as investment ceases to increase, exaggerated pessimism will take the place of exaggerated optimism and the slump period will be inaugurated by a sudden violent decline in activity instead of a gradual relapse.

The rhythm of thriftiness and the rhythm of expectations exaggerate the effects of the rhythm of investment. Movements of the rate of interest on the other hand come in as a counterweight to the rest. As the level of activity

93

declines the demand for money shrinks, and the rate of interest tends to fall. The decline in investment is therefore less severe than it would be if the rate of interest were constant, and when the bottom is reached recovery sets in sooner. Conversely, increasing activity, particularly if it is accompanied by rising money wages, drives up the rate of interest by increasing the demand for money. Consequently the increase in the rate of investment is checked and the period of prosperity curtailed. Thus the rhythm of the rate of interest runs counter to the rhythm of investment and damps down the oscillations of trade.

A movement, in either direction, in one country tends to spread over the world. Booms and slumps are catching, for when activity increases in one country the benefit is felt in others, by way of increased demand for exports, and when activity falls off in one country the rest are impoverished. For any one country the initial upward movement may take the form of increased foreign investment due to a revival of activity abroad.

A movement in the exchange rate may counteract influences coming from the outside world and the infection spreads most easily when the exchanges are stable. When the gold standard system was in full operation the nations of the western economic world moved closely in step with each other, but in the post-war period we have several times seen particular countries insulated from a world slump by a reduced exchange rate, or cut off from the benefits of a world revival by pertinacious adherence to a high rate.

CONTROLLING THE TRADE CYCLE

These movements comprise what is often called the " natural " rhythm of business activity, as opposed to the influences of government or monetary policy. The dichotomy is somewhat artificial, for the actions of governments and monetary authorities are as much a part of nature as the actions of private entrepreneurs ; but the world is growing more conscious of the trade cycle, it is beginning to be regarded as a duty for the authorities to mitigate the violence of booms and slumps by whatever means they may possess, and their actions therefore tend to run counter to the action of private entrepreneurs.

The motive of the authorities for attempting to improve trade during a slump is obvious enough. There are two distinct types of motive for wishing to check a boom. First, it is often argued that boom conditions should be prevented from developing because it is the boom which is the cause of the slump that follows it. In a certain sense this is true, for as we have seen it is the very fact that a high rate of capital accumulation takes place in the boom which prevents the boom from continuing. But it does not follow that booms ought to be eliminated. There are not two kinds of investment — good investment which does not bring on a decline in activity and bad investment which does. All investment is good in that it promotes activity while it is going on and adds to wealth when it is completed. All is bad in the sense that it cannot last and must be followed by a decline in activity. It is impossible to get rid of the bad features of investment without sacrificing the good features, and to stabilise trade by means of eliminating booms would merely be to enforce a permanent slump. It may, indeed, be argued that the average of prosperity, one year with another, would be higher if a moderate level of prosperity were exchanged for a high level at some times and a low level at others, though, even if this could be established, a policy of maintaining unemployment permanently at a little below its present average level is not one that can be recommended with much enthusiasm. But whatever may be the merits of the argument, the notion that a boom is to be feared as a cause of depression has considerable influence in inclining the authorities to check the development of boom conditions when they begin to appear.

The second motive for wishing to damp down boom conditions is the fear of inflation. Inflation has become a stock bogy to such an extent that even in the depths of depression in 1931 it was not thought ridiculous to frighten the public by parading it, but actually no case of extreme inflation has been known to occur in normal circumstances. Inflation as we have seen requires two conditions : first, that the level of unemployment has fallen so low that a violent and irresistible rise in money wages takes place ; and second, that something has occurred to remove the stopper normally provided by a limited quantity of money, which ensures that the rate of interest shall be pushed up, and investment consequently checked, when the rise in money wages begins. Wars and revolutions have frequently led to violent inflation, but in times of peace with a stable government and a competent monetary authority it is little to be feared. All the same the dread of inflation has such a strong hold upon the minds of the authorities that it plays an important part in inclining them to use their influence to prevent trade conditions from becoming what they regard as dangerously good.

Apart from beggar-my-neighbour policies, the two chief weapons of the authorities for counteracting booms and slumps are the rate of interest and public investment. The monetary authorities normally try to foster the remedial action of the rate of interest by deliberately increasing the quantity of money when activity has fallen to a low level, and restricting it when the boom is at its height, thus enhancing the " natural " movements in the rate of interest. It is found that such action as the authorities normally take is not sufficient to induce a steady rate of investment, for once pessimism has taken hold of the entrepreneurs a moderate fall in the rate of interest is not sufficient to restore the inducement to invest, and when they are dazzled by golden visions of profit a moderate rise in the rate of interest will not check their enthusiasm. But the movements of the rate of interest induced by the authorities at least tell in the direction of damping down oscillations of trade.

Public works policy has long been advocated as a corrective to the trade cycle. The ideal policy which has been put forward is for plans to be worked out many years in advance of requirements, and for the rate at which they are carried out to be adjusted so as to counteract the movements of private investment. This policy has now won almost universal acceptance in principle but it has yet to be seen in full action. A considerable share in the revival of trade which began in 1933 is to be attributed to the deliberate efforts of a number of governments to foster investment. But in the early part of 1937, when talk of a boom began to be common and a reduction in public investment was advocated, the governments of the world were concentrating their energies on an armaments race, so that public investment increased still further just at the time when a revival in private investment was well under way.

LONG-PERIOD INFLUENCES

The regular pattern of the trade cycle is interrupted by particular events — a war, a good harvest, a political crisis, an important invention or the discovery of a new gold-field — which jerk the movement of trade from its

97

normal course, so that the path which it follows is full of irregularities. The history of trade presents the spectacle of a strong tendency to regular oscillations, interrupted by sporadic movements in one direction or another.

Further, the oscillations of the trade cycle overlie deeper influences. Increasing population, a rapid succession of inventions and opportunities for exploiting new territories, give buoyancy to the profitability of capital and provide an ever-renewed stimulus to investment.

When these sources of demand for capital are lacking it appears that the motive for investment must be chronically weak, so that slumps are deep and prolonged, and moderate prosperity is hailed by contrast as a boom. Since the increase in population is rapidly approaching its end in the western world, no fresh continents remain to be discovered, and a new age of invention comparable with the nineteenth century is scarcely to be hoped for, it appears that in the near future powerful stimulants will have to be applied to the economic system if chronic unemployment is to be avoided.

A long-run fall in the rate of interest would do much to stimulate private investment, while an extension of public investment could make up for its deficiencies, and a drastic policy of redistribution of income would increase consumption, and reduce the amount of investment necessary to preserve a reasonable level of employment. All these policies meet with serious difficulties and have to contend with violent opposition, and it remains to be seen whether it is possible for the present economic system to adapt itself to the requirements of the future.

CHAPTER XIII

CONTROVERSY IN ECONOMICS

Types of Controversy

THE subject-matter of this book has been the battle-ground of controversy since thinking about economic affairs first began, and the controversy is still raging. But in a subject of this sort there can be no ground for controversy. Differences of opinion there may be, but all controversies should be capable of resolution. The rules of logic and the laws of evidence are the same for everyone, and in the nature of the case there can be nothing to dispute about.

Controversies arise for five main reasons. First, they occur when the two parties fail to understand each other. Here patience and toleration should provide a cure. Second, controversies occur in which one (or both) of the parties has made an error of logic. Here the spectators at least should be able to decide on which side reason lies. Third, the two parties may be making, unwittingly, different assumptions, and each maintaining something which is correct on the appropriate assumptions. The two knights are disputing as to whether the shield is black or white, when one side of the shield is black and the other side white. Here the remedy is to discover the assumptions and to set each argument out in a manner which makes clear that it is not inconsistent with the other. Fourth, there may not be sufficient evidence to settle a question of fact conclusively one way or the other. Here the remedy is for each party to preserve an open mind and to assist in the search for further evidence. Fifth, there may be differences of opinion as to what is a desirable state of affairs. Here no resolution is possible, since judgments of ultimate values cannot be settled by any purely intellectual process. But dispute is idle.

It is the fifth source of controversy which keeps all the rest alive. When some important issue of public policy is at stake each disputant clings desperately to his own opinion. Each refuses to understand the other, for fear that if he understood he might be compelled to make some concession. Each persists in his errors, for he who is convinced against his will is of the same opinion still. Each refuses to reconsider his assumptions for fear of being obliged to admit that his assumptions do not conform to reality. Each reads the incomplete evidence in his own favour.

Controversies in economics persist, not because economists are necessarily less intelligent or more bad-tempered than the rest of mankind, but because the issues involved arouse strong feeling. A bad argument which appears to favour a desired policy is obstinately and passionately upheld in the face of a better argument that appears to tell against it. But argument in the nature of the case can make no difference to ultimate judgments based on interest or moral feeling. The ideal is to set out all the arguments fairly on their merits, and agree to differ about ultimate values.

SOURCES OF CONTROVERSY

On questions of policy the differences can never be resolved. Even such an apparently simple problem as, for instance, the extension of public works as a remedy for unemployment, is found to give rise to violent conflicts of interest.

It appears at first sight as though, if governments can reduce unemployment, and add to real wealth, by undertaking investment, it must be quite unambiguously beneficial for them to do so. But even on this question acute differences of opinion arise. We have seen that the community as a whole is enriched by public works undertaken during a slump. But many individuals in the community find that they suffer from such a policy. Those who are enriched by additional saving during the periods of profits induced by public works are not necessarily, man for man, the same individuals who will have to pay higher taxes in the future to provide interest on the larger public debt. Anyone who shares more (or fears he may share more) in the additional future taxation than in the additional present profit will have a motive for opposing the scheme. Individuals whose incomes are legally fixed in terms of money suffer from a rise of prices when employment increases. Governments who are opposed in principle to extending the sphere of socialism prefer that there should be less real capital in existence rather than that they should be saddled with the ownership of more capital. Revolutionaries who regard unemployment as only one of the evils of a system of private enterprise are not anxious for capitalist governments to learn the trick of reducing fluctuations in trade, and so deprive them of the most obvious, though not the most fundamental, of their objections to the system. The adherents of *laisser-faire*, on the other hand, fear that, if it once became clear to the public that state interference can reduce unemployment, the public might begin to think that state interference could do much else besides.

All these conflicts are raised even by the simple question of public works policy. How much the more by questions involving reductions in inequality of income.

Academic disputes amongst economists are apt to appear to the layman as idle and remote as the dispute as to how many angels can stand on a pin. But the academic disputes about x's and y's are in reality the surface ripples of these deep-lying conflicts (if they were not so, all the questions would have been settled long ago). The controversies and the political issues are bound up together. Both have been avoided as far as possible in this book.

INDEX

Potage à l'oignon

The French Kitchen

A Cookbook

THE FRENCH KITCHEN

A Cookbook

Joanne Harris and Fran Warde

Doubleday

LONDON · NEW YORK · TORONTO · SYDNEY · AUCKLAND

Transworld Publishers
61–63 Uxbridge Road, London W5 5SA
a division of The Random House Group Ltd

Random House Australia (PTY) Ltd
20 Alfred Street, Milsons Point, Sydney,
New South Wales 2061, Australia

Random House New Zealand Ltd
18 Poland Road, Glenfield, Auckland 10, New Zealand

Random House South Africa (PTY) Ltd
Endulini, 5a Jubilee Road, Parktown 2193, South Africa

Published 2002 by Doubleday
a division of Transworld Publishers

A catalogue record for this book is available
from the British Library.
ISBN 0385 604769

Photography by Debi Treloar
Designed by Carroll Associates

Printed by Appl Druck, Wemding, Germany

Introduction

Many of my earliest memories are about food. I remember making pancakes with Mémée, my great-grandmother, in her house in Vitré when I was three years old. I remember making jam with my grandfather in Barnsley, and picking blackberries to make wine. I remember my Yorkshire grandmother's rhubarb and apple pie, and my French grandmother's green fig jam. I remember long childhood holidays on the island of Noirmoutier, going round the markets in the early morning or cooking sardines on a charcoal brazier on the sand, and I remember *poule au pot* in Gascony with my grandfather's old friends the Douazans. So many memories are associated with the tastes and smells of cooking; so many places, so many people can be brought to life using nothing more than a handful of herbs or an old recipe.

It's astonishing how much of our past and our culture is secretly defined by food. Our earliest sensations are to do with tastes and smells; as infants we experience food as comfort, food as an expression of love. Later we make our own associations, but for me, the kitchen has always been the heart of my family, a place where the family assembles, not just to eat, but to be together, to talk, to put the world to rights, to teach, to remember the past, to watch and learn.

My kitchen is essentially French in character. There's a strong tradition of cooking on my French side, handed down from my great-grandmother. My mother, too, is a terrific cook, and when she arrived in Yorkshire – speaking virtually no English and feeling, inevitably, a little homesick – she used the familiar recipes to remember the people at home, to remind herself of who she was, and to keep in touch with her cultural identity.

As far as I know, my father had no difficulty in adjusting to this radical change of diet. However, married as I am to a vegetarian (and with a militant 8-year-old veggie daughter), I have discovered that sometimes cultures clash. Not that I have anything against vegetarianism. I enjoy vegetarian food, and when I am at home I rarely cook anything else. But food is as much about heritage as it is about taste; and the French half of me refuses to let go of so large a section of my past. As a result, this book is a kind of family album, in which every recipe paints a picture, as well as, I hope, an introduction to some of the regional flavours of France.

Cooking is a social activity. My mother's kitchen – and my grandmother's, and my great-grandmother's – was open to all comers. My grandmother sang constantly (and very tunelessly) as she peeled potatoes. My mother told stories.

There were forbidden areas (my great-aunt Marinette's pancake pan, for instance, was formally out of bounds), but for the most part the kitchen was a learning zone for children, a place where philosophies were expounded, histories examined and scandals unearthed. Inevitably, much of my childhood seems to have taken place in and around kitchens. The recipes in this book are mostly French because my main influences come from there, mostly traditional because they have been handed down over many years, and mostly very simple to make. When the ingredients are really good, simple food works; there is no need for complicated sauces or fiddly garnishes. Traditional food demands respect and attention to quality, and this, I think, is the principal ingredient of the French kitchen.

Regardless of other differences, on this subject my English and my French sides are in complete agreement. Food – and its preparation – should be a pleasure. Faced with such a bewildering selection of 'conveniently' processed foods and ready meals in the supermarkets, it is sometimes hard to remember this. There is nothing convenient about bad food. When in a hurry, it still takes less time to make a fabulous salad or sandwich or pasta dish than it does to defrost an overpriced tray of mush. So take a little time in selecting your ingredients; go out of your way to find a really good organic butcher or cheesemonger or baker. Visit markets instead of supermarkets. Rediscover the joy of eating locally grown produce in season, instead of food flown in from the other side of the world. Try growing your own herbs (lack of space is no excuse – even a window-ledge will do). If you are lucky enough to have a garden, then you may already have discovered the difference between home-grown and far-flown; if not, try a couple of life-enhancing rows of carrots or spinach or raspberries or a pot of some impossible-to-find species of tomato. Brought up alongside my grandfather's allotment in Yorkshire, I developed this addiction to home-grown food early in life, and I am still amazed at the number of people who think that tomatoes are round and red and tasteless (as opposed to green and sweet and stripy, or long and yellow and tangy, or orange and lumpy and fantastic), or that most unidentified things taste like chicken, or that strawberries have a uniform shape. Food is a sensual, whole-body experience: look at what you are cooking, smell the ingredients, mix them with your fingers. Enjoy their sounds and textures. Bear in mind that cooking is about as close to magic as modern society allows: to take a set of basic ingredients and to transform them into something wonderful, something from another part of the world. Most of all, have fun. Bring your friends into the kitchen; ask your family to help. Let your children watch. Enjoy it together.

Salads

Many people on seeing the word 'salad' in a cookbook will tend to shudder and pass quickly on to the section marked 'chocolate'. This is because for many years salads have had a rather bad press, and have been associated mainly with dieting and the depression that often follows. However, French salads take us far beyond these stereotypical wet-lettuce-and-celery-stick meals and into an area of vast and delicious diversity. For a start, salads do not have to contain lettuce. They do not even have to contain vegetables, although they do provide a wonderful means of making the most of the seasonal fruits and vegetables that are one of the principal beauties of a French market. Salads may be served warm or cold and contain raw or cooked ingredients, but will most often be served with some form of dressing, usually containing lemon juice, vinegar, oil and spices.

I remember being taught to prepare French dressing when I was about four years old – it's that easy. To three tablespoons of oil, add one of vinegar, plus another of mustard. Salt and pepper to taste, then mix well with a fork. You can use other ingredients to vary the taste: balsamic or grainy mustard, herbs, chillies, garlic or different types of oil and vinegar. The results can be dramatically different; walnut or pistachio oil, for instance, give an entirely different flavour to a goat's cheese salad, or try adding a splash of raspberry vinegar to a summer salad for a fresh, sweeter taste.

The beauty of salads is that the variations are almost endless. Crisp leaves and herbs, sliced fruit, grated carrots, seeds, olives, cheeses, warm potatoes with olive oil, capers and garlic dressing, marinated duck or salted fish – all these work very well, and you can vary your combinations according to the season or to suit your personal taste. They are extremely easy to prepare, and for the most part, very quick, and it is for this reason that I make so many salads, both in winter and in summer. My favourites are among the simplest: raw cep (porcini) mushrooms, thinly sliced and served with lemon, a little salt and a drizzle of olive oil; fat ripe tomatoes, warmed on a sunny window-ledge and served sliced with French dressing and chopped parsley; grated carrots, with parsley, oil and lemon. These are the most basic of recipes, but they can be truly spectacular if the ingredients are good enough, and serve to remind us how wonderful some foods can be with only a minimum of fuss and preparation.

Salads are easy, quick and endlessly variable.
Despite being among the most basic of recipes, the
results can be wonderful: as good on the eye as on
the tongue. The better the ingredients, the better the
results, so shop carefully, or grow your own.

I adore this dish. It's so simple, but the flavours and smells of it take me right back to holidays in France by the sea, and to the little goat farm on Noirmoutier where my mother always bought our cheeses.

16

Warm Goat's Cheese Salad

There are different types of goat's cheese – such as the delightfully named *crottins de chèvre* – but for this recipe it's better to use the *bûche* or log-shaped cheeses. There is a wonderfully earthy taste to good goat's cheese, which, when mixed with really fresh salad leaves, crunchy walnuts and good, spicy olives, evokes the spirit of summer.

Preparation: 10 minutes
Cooking: 5 minutes

Serves 6

300g goat's cheese log: the best you can find
6 slices of baguette
200g mixed salad leaves
50g walnuts
100g black niçoise olives, pitted

For the dressing:
1 tsp grainy mustard
1 tsp Dijon mustard
2 tbsp cider vinegar
sea salt
freshly ground black pepper
6 tbsp extra-virgin olive oil

Heat the grill to high.

Cut the goat's cheese into six ½cm slices and put one on top of each slice of baguette. Put on the grill tray, but not under the grill yet.

Put the mustards, cider vinegar and seasoning in a jam jar and shake vigorously until smooth. Add the olive oil and shake again to blend. Pour the dressing into a mixing bowl, add the leaves, walnuts and olives, and toss well. Put the goat's cheese under the grill and cook for 2 minutes until the cheese is colouring and bubbling. Serve at once on a bed of salad.

Wild Mushroom Salad

If you can't find ceps (often known by their Italian name, porcini), use other wild varieties, such as horn of plenty, chanterelle and morel, or good cultivated mushrooms.

Preparation: 10 minutes
Cooking: 20 minutes

Serves 6

6 medium-sized cep mushrooms
olive oil for frying
200g thick-cut bacon, diced (see the note: right)
100ml white wine
1 tbsp balsamic vinegar
3 cloves of garlic, crushed, peeled and chopped
a sprinkling of paprika
a bunch of flat-leaf parsley, chopped
sea salt
freshly ground black pepper
300g mixed salad leaves
2 tbsp extra-virgin olive oil
6 thin slices of toast

Break the stalks of the mushrooms away from the caps, trim the ends and brush away any dirt. Don't wash the mushrooms.

Heat a little olive oil in a large pan, add the mushroom stalks and caps, and cook for 5 minutes until golden brown. Remove the mushrooms from the pan with a slotted spoon, add the bacon and cook until golden. Then return the mushrooms along with the wine, balsamic vinegar, garlic, paprika, parsley and seasoning, and simmer for 8 minutes, adding a little water if the liquid evaporates and the pan threatens to become dry.

Meanwhile, toss the salad leaves in the extra-virgin olive oil. Put the toasts on a plate, cover with the salad leaves and serve the mushrooms on top with any juice from the pan drizzled over.

A little bacon fried in a pan not only renders fat but
also adds flavour. You need good, thick-cut bacon.
Don't bother with pre-sliced: it's too skinny. Buy
thick-cut from your butcher, or get a 500g piece
(I use smoked), keep it in the fridge, and cut off
1.5cm strips when needed. Remove the skin and
dice the flesh into perfect chunks of bacon.

Haricots Blancs en Salade: a perfect light meal on its own as well as the ideal accompaniment to more elaborate dishes. The haricot beans have a wonderful, slightly floury texture that is ideal for use in salads: they absorb flavours and melt in the mouth. Don't add salt during cooking, though – it toughens the skins.

White Haricot Bean and Tomato Salad

Haricots Blancs en Salade goes really well with grilled fillets of fish, turning a simple dish into something special.

Preparation: 30 minutes,
plus overnight soaking if using dried beans
Cooking: 30 minutes

Serves 6

2 x 410g tins white haricot beans, drained,
or 200g dried white haricot beans
400g new potatoes
400g ripe tomatoes
4 spring onions, finely sliced
a bunch of flat-leaf parsley, roughly chopped
1 red chilli, finely diced (include the seeds
if you like it hot)
4 tbsp extra-virgin olive oil
zest and juice of 1 lemon
sea salt
freshly ground black pepper

If you're using dried beans, soak them overnight in a saucepan of cold water. The next day, drain them, rinse well and return to the pan. Cover with water, bring to the boil and simmer for 1 hour. Skim off any froth that rises to the top during cooking. Drain and cool.

Cook the potatoes in their skins in a pan of simmering water for 20 minutes. Drain and allow to cool, then cut into wedges. Dip the tomatoes in a pan of boiling water for 20 seconds, peel, cut into wedges and remove the seeds. Mix the potatoes, tomatoes and drained beans together.

Combine the spring onions, parsley and chilli with the olive oil, lemon juice, zest and seasoning. Pour over the tomatoes, beans and potatoes, mix well and serve immediately.

Green Bean Salad with Pine Nuts and Feta

This is a cheerful, easy-to-make salad – *Haricots en Fête* – which my vegetarian husband can eat as a main course without feeling too left out.

Preparation: 15 minutes
Cooking: 5 minutes

Serves 6

400g green beans, topped and tailed
50g pine nuts
200g feta cheese, crumbled
a bunch of flat-leaf parsley, finely chopped
100g olives
4 tbsp extra-virgin olive oil
juice of 1 lemon
sea salt
freshly ground black pepper

Plunge the beans into a pan of boiling water, cook for 2 minutes, then drain and refresh in cold water until the beans are cold. Drain and dry them and place in a large salad bowl.

Cook the pine nuts in a non-stick pan over a medium heat until golden all over. Be warned: nothing seems to happen for a while then all of a sudden the pine nuts will colour very quickly. Add the pine nuts to the beans along with the feta, flat-leaf parsley, olives, olive oil, lemon juice and seasoning. Mix well and serve at once.

Tuna and Warm Potato Salad

This is a fabulous salad for winter or summer, full of different textures and rich flavours. Excellent as a main course – try serving it in a large dish in the centre of the table, with plenty of crusty bread.

Preparation: 30 minutes
Cooking: 30 minutes

Serves 6

500g small new potatoes
olive oil for coating
250g cherry tomatoes
200g fine green beans, topped and tailed
200g tuna in olive oil, drained
4 anchovies, cut lengthways into thin strips
(see note: right)
1 large bunch of basil

For the dressing:
2 shallots, finely diced
3 tbsp white wine vinegar
2 tbsp grainy mustard (such as Meaux)
sea salt
freshly ground black pepper
7 tbsp extra-virgin olive oil

Gently cook the potatoes in their skins in a pan of simmering water for 20 minutes.

Heat the oven to 200°C/gas 6. Lightly brush a baking tray with olive oil. Toss the cherry tomatoes in the oil to coat them and roast in the hot oven for 10 minutes.

Put the dressing ingredients, except the oil, into a jar with a tight-fitting lid and shake until well blended. Then add the olive oil and shake vigorously again.

Drain the potatoes, cut them in half and place in a salad bowl. Pour the dressing over and toss to coat the warm potatoes.

Plunge the green beans into boiling water and cook for 2 minutes. Drain well and add, warm, to the potatoes. Flake and add the tuna along with the anchovy strips and the tomatoes straight from the oven, and gently mix. Tear up the basil, scatter it over the salad and serve at once.

A small but key part of this dish is the anchovy. Tiny fish that are abundant in the Mediterranean, they are rarely found fresh but are instead sold preserved in salt or olive oil, either whole or in fillets. Look out for salt-preserved anchovies. They are less easy to find, but they are the best. Once the jar or tin is opened, store anchovies in the fridge.

I like to keep an open mind when shopping for food. Markets are the best places in which to find beautiful, fresh vegetables and salad ingredients, so be creative, and let yourself be seduced by what is on display.

Frisée with *Lardons*

Frisée lettuces are one of the joys of a French summer market. As large and curly as a bouquet of chrysanthemums, they have a lovely texture and more taste than ordinary lettuces. The combination of fresh lettuce, fried *lardons* (bacon cubes) and warm, creamy poached-egg topping is cheery and irresistible.

Preparation: 15 minutes
Cooking: 30 minutes

Serves 6

1 large frisée lettuce
2 shallots, diced
olive oil for frying
½ baguette, cut into cubes
500g thick-cut bacon, cubed
6 farm fresh eggs
2 tbsp red wine vinegar
2 tbsp Dijon mustard
sea salt
freshly ground black pepper
2 tbsp extra-virgin olive oil

Break up the frisée lettuce, wash and spin it dry, and place in a large bowl with the shallots. Heat a little olive oil in a frying pan and fry the bread in batches until golden on all sides, then remove from the pan and place on kitchen paper. Wipe out the pan, add a little more olive oil and fry the bacon for 8 minutes or until golden.

To poach the eggs to perfection, bring a pan of water to a gentle simmer. Carefully break in the eggs, return the water to a simmer, then immediately remove the pan from the heat. Cover it with a lid and leave to sit for 5 minutes.

Put the red wine vinegar and Dijon mustard along with the seasoning into a jar with a tight-fitting lid and shake vigorously to combine. Add the olive oil and shake again. Pour over the lettuce and toss well. Add the golden bread cubes and bacon to the salad and toss. Serve on individual plates, each salad topped with a hot poached egg.

Artichokes with Vinaigrette

Artichauts Vinaigrette is a dish for people who have plenty of time to eat it – and by the time you reach the tender hearts of the artichokes, I can guarantee that any ice between yourself and your dinner companions will have been well and truly broken!

Preparation: 10 minutes
Cooking: 40 minutes

Serves 6

6 globe artichokes, prepared as shown

For the vinaigrette:
2 tsp Dijon mustard
1/2 tsp unrefined caster sugar
sea salt
freshly ground black pepper
juice of 1/2 lemon
2 tbsp white wine vinegar
6 tbsp extra-virgin olive oil

Bring a large pan of water to the boil. Put the artichokes in the boiling water – sit a colander on top of the pan to submerge them – and simmer for 30–40 minutes. The leaves should break away easily when the artichoke is cooked. Remove the artichokes and drain upside down to release all the water.

Meanwhile, make the vinaigrette: place the mustard, sugar, seasoning, lemon juice and vinegar in a large jar with a tight-fitting lid and shake vigorously until blended. Add the oil and shake vigorously until a smooth vinaigrette has formed.

If you know your friends like vinaigrette, pour it over the artichokes before serving. Alternatively, serve the vinaigrette in a little dish for dipping. Peel away the leaves and eat the soft nodule, pulling it off the leaf with your teeth. When you get to the base of the artichoke, in one firm tug pull away the hairy cluster (the choke) and discard it, and eat the sumptuous heart.

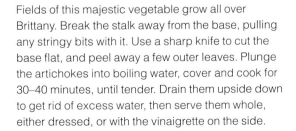

Fields of this majestic vegetable grow all over Brittany. Break the stalk away from the base, pulling any stringy bits with it. Use a sharp knife to cut the base flat, and peel away a few outer leaves. Plunge the artichokes into boiling water, cover and cook for 30–40 minutes, until tender. Drain them upside down to get rid of excess water, then serve them whole, either dressed, or with the vinaigrette on the side.

Basil and Rocket Salad with Melting Tomatoes

This is a lovely, simple salad in which the smoky flavour of the roasted tomatoes contrasts beautifully with the sweetness of the basil and the pepperiness of the rocket leaves.

Preparation: 20 minutes
Cooking: 10 minutes

Serves 6

olive oil for roasting
200g cherry tomatoes
2 tbsp extra-virgin olive oil
juice of 1 lemon
1 tsp balsamic mustard
200g fresh basil leaves
200g fresh rocket leaves

Heat the oven to 200°C/gas 6.

Drizzle a little olive oil over a small roasting pan, add the tomatoes and put in the oven to cook for 10 minutes until they just begin to brown.

Put the extra-virgin olive oil in a salad bowl, add the lemon juice and balsamic mustard and blend together. Add the basil and rocket and toss until all the leaves are coated. Top with the hot tomatoes and serve at once.

Aïoli with Herbs

Use this versatile sauce as a dip for raw vegetables, or as an accompaniment to grilled fish. Replace the herbs with a finely chopped chilli to make a hot spicy sauce: great with bouillabaisse.

Preparation: 20 minutes

Serves 6

4 egg yolks
1 tbsp white wine vinegar
1/2 tsp dry mustard
2 tbsp water
6 cloves of garlic, crushed, peeled and finely diced
sea salt
freshly ground black pepper
500ml extra-virgin olive oil
a bunch of chives, finely chopped
a bunch of dill, finely chopped

Whisk together the egg yolks, vinegar, dry mustard and water using an electric hand-held mixer or a blender. (You have to work hard if you do it by hand.) Add the garlic along with the salt and pepper, and blend again. Slowly pour in the olive oil, mixing constantly to emulsify the eggs and make a mayonnaise-style sauce. If the mixture is too thick, add a little extra water to adjust the consistency.

Stir the chopped herbs in well. Store in the fridge and use within 3 days.

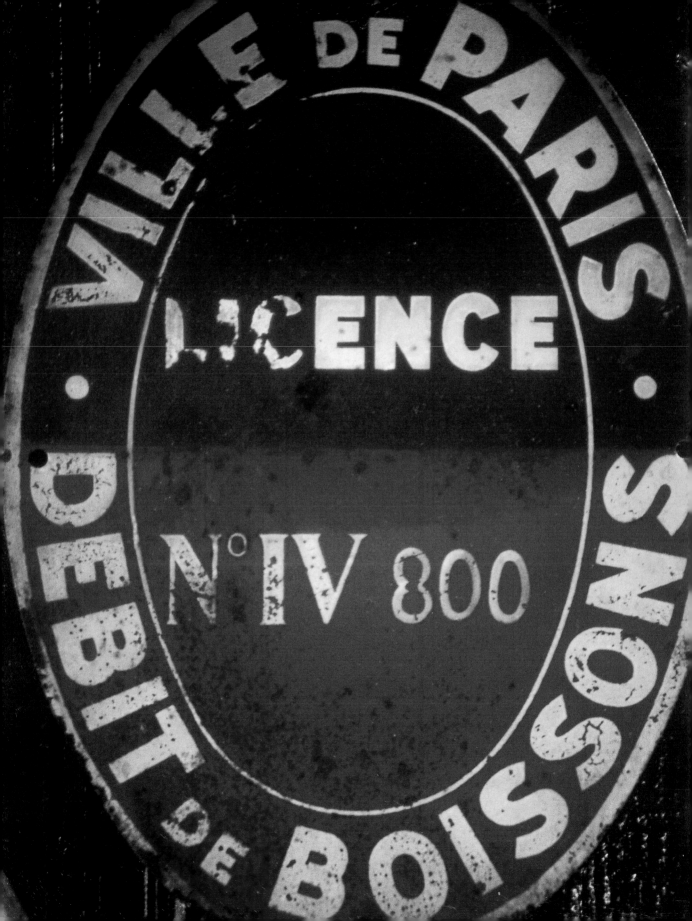

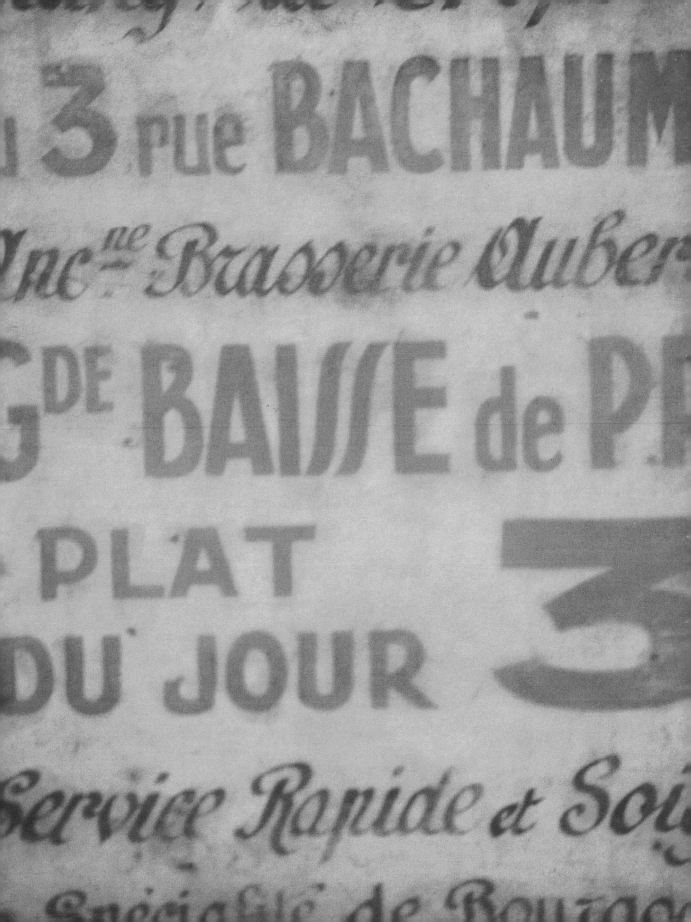

Soups & Savouries

Originally, soups tended to be served at the beginning of the evening meal. There are many types, from clear *consommés* and *bouillons*, which are light and delicate, to the peasant stews like *pot-au-feu* or *poule au pot*, which are hearty enough to make up an entire meal.

I love making soups because they are so easy and versatile, and because of their comforting childhood associations, although a really elegant light soup is also a terrific way of starting a celebratory dinner.

Some of the savouries in this chapter are adaptations of main courses which, depending on the occasion, can also be served in smaller portions as *hors-d'oeuvres*. However, most French *hors-d'oeuvres* are very simple, designed only to stimulate the appetite for the next course. Typically, try selections of any of the following:

radishes served with fresh butter and sea salt
tomatoes, sliced and salted, with chopped herbs and vinaigrette dressing
marinated olives in oil
half a melon, served with port
grated carrots, tossed in oil, lemon, sea salt and pepper
charcuterie: a selection of pâté, sausage, smoked ham and so on, served with pickled gherkins

The simplest meals are often the best. Try a rich, comforting home-made soup, served with lots of good bread – this is real fast food, good for all generations. Add a bottle of wine for the adults …

Don't be put off by the amount of garlic in this
recipe. Roasted garlic has a mellow, sweet flavour,
a creamy texture and an irresistible aroma. Roast
the garlic cloves in their skins and then, when cool
enough to handle, squeeze the lovely flesh out. And
once you've conquered your garlic fears here, try
Great-aunt Simone's Garlic Soup on page 40.

Gascony Tomato Soup

This rich, sweet soup – *Soupe de Tomates à la Gasconne* – relies on the traditional ingredients of Gascony for its powerful flavour. Serve with warm French bread.

Preparation: 30 minutes
Cooking: 2 hours

Serves 6

400g cherry tomatoes
4 whole garlic bulbs, cut in half crossways
olive oil
sea salt
freshly ground black pepper
200g mixed wild mushrooms, sliced
1 red onion, diced
100ml red wine
2 sprigs of rosemary
1 bay leaf
1 litre vegetable stock
a bunch of flat-leaf parsley, chopped

Heat the oven to 150°C/gas 2.

Put the cherry tomatoes and halved garlic bulbs in a roasting pan with a little olive oil and seasoning, toss well to coat in oil then roast in the oven for 40 minutes. Remove from the oven and allow to cool.

Heat a drizzle of olive oil in a saucepan, add the mushrooms and red onion, and cook over a medium heat for 5 minutes. Add the red wine, rosemary, bay leaf and vegetable stock and gently simmer for 10 minutes.

When cool enough to handle, slip the garlic flesh out of its skin, then add it along with the tomatoes to the mushroom mix. Simmer gently for a further hour – do not boil. Add parsley just before serving.

Butternut Soup

This is a lovely way of using butternut squash, which has a sweet, subtle flavour and a meltingly tender consistency when properly cooked.

Preparation: 25 minutes
Cooking: 45 minutes

Serves 6

1.5kg butternut squash
2 tbsp olive oil
50g butter
2 onions, peeled and chopped
2 cloves of garlic, crushed, peeled and chopped
1 tsp curry powder
sea salt
freshly ground black pepper
1.5 litres vegetable or chicken stock
a bunch of flat-leaf parsley, finely chopped

Butternuts are one of the hardest vegetables to cut. Always use a large sharp knife. The easiest way is to top and tail the butternut, then cut it across into two. Stand each half on one end and cut away the skin from top to bottom. Halve each piece lengthways and remove the seeds.
Heat the oil and butter in a large saucepan, add the onions and garlic and gently sauté.

While the onions and garlic are sautéing, chop the butternut flesh, then add it to the onions and mix well. Stir in the curry powder and seasoning. Pour in the stock, stir well and bring to the boil. Simmer for 35 minutes until the butternut is soft.

Blend the soup with a hand-held blender (a worthwhile purchase, by the way, if you don't have one already). Serve topped with plenty of parsley and a drizzle of olive oil.

Onion Soup

Subtle, smoky-flavoured *Soupe à l'Oignon* is associated with the *réveillon* on Christmas Eve, and is a traditional winter favourite. Alexandre Dumas, in his *Grand Dictionnaire de la Cuisine*, tells the story of how King Stanislas, a noted gourmet, was served such a delicious onion soup while visiting his daughter and son-in-law in Versailles that he refused to leave without a demonstration of the recipe. Dumas describes the king in his dressing-gown, a scarf around his head, tears running down his face as he watched the chef at work. Of course, this may just have been the onions …

Preparation: 30 minutes
Cooking: 1 hour 30 minutes

Serves 6

50g butter
750g onions, finely sliced (using a mandolin cutter is the easiest way)
3 cloves of garlic, crushed, peeled and chopped
25g flour
1.5 litres beef or vegetable stock
200ml white wine
1 bay leaf
a sprig of thyme
sea salt
freshly ground black pepper
a bunch of curly parsley, finely chopped
1/2 baguette, cut into 1cm slices
100g Gruyère cheese, finely grated

Melt the butter in a large saucepan, add the onions and cook on a low heat for 50 minutes, stirring frequently. The onions should turn a golden brown, be very soft and begin to caramelize, which gives this soup its rich golden colour and deep flavour.

Add the garlic along with the flour and mix well to allow the flour to absorb the excess butter, making a roux. Slowly pour in the stock and wine, stirring frequently, then bring to a gentle simmer. Add the bay leaf, thyme leaves (strip them from the sprig), salt and pepper, cover with a lid and leave for 40 minutes on a low heat. Five minutes before serving, add the parsley to the soup and stir well. Toast the slices of baguette and top with the grated Gruyère. Then grill the toast until the cheese is melted. Serve the soup in bowls topped with the cheesy toasts.

To me this bean soup smells of my grandmother's garden in spring. It is a wonderful way to make the most of young, home-grown vegetables if you are lucky enough to have them.

Bean Soup with *Pistou*

This is a light and evocative dish, filled with the tastes, colours and scents of approaching summer. It is extremely therapeutic to make, especially if you make the *pistou* by hand.

Preparation: 30 minutes, plus overnight soaking
Cooking: 50 minutes

Serves 6

125g dried red haricot beans
125g dried white haricot beans
1 tbsp olive oil
1 onion, diced
2 sticks of celery, finely chopped
1 leek, finely chopped
2 potatoes, diced
1 carrot, diced
1.5 litres vegetable or chicken stock
sea salt
freshly ground black pepper
4 tomatoes
125g French green beans, trimmed
1 courgette
4 artichoke hearts
100g vermicelli

For the *pistou*:
6 cloves of garlic, crushed, peeled
and roughly chopped
a generous bunch of basil
75ml extra-virgin olive oil
sea salt
freshly ground black pepper

Soak the beans overnight in a saucepan of cold water. The next day, drain them, rinse well and return to the pan. Cover with water, bring to the boil and simmer for 1 hour. Skim off any froth that rises to the top during cooking. Drain and set aside.

Then make the *pistou*. You can make it by hand in a pestle and mortar, or use a small blender. Combine the garlic and basil leaves until they have almost formed a paste. Slowly mix in the olive oil, add the seasoning and place to one side.

To make the soup, heat the olive oil in a saucepan and sauté the onion, celery, leek, potatoes and carrot over a medium-low heat for 20 minutes without browning them. Add the vegetable stock, haricot beans and seasoning, and simmer for 20 minutes.

Meanwhile, score the skin of the tomatoes and plunge them into a pan of boiling water for 10 seconds, then remove and peel away the skin. Cut into quarters, remove the seeds and dice the remaining flesh. Cut the beans into 2.5cm lengths, finely dice the courgette and slice the artichoke hearts into quarters. Add to the simmering soup along with the vermicelli and tomato and cook for 10 more minutes. Serve with a spoonful of the *pistou* on top of each bowl.

Great-aunt Simone's Garlic Soup

Soupe à l'Ail Simone Sorin is one of the great memory dishes of my childhood. During my summer holidays on Noirmoutier, my great-aunt Simone and great-uncle Jean would come to spend a few days with us. On her arrival, Simone, who is an enthusiastic cook, would often prepare this dish, one of her favourites. However far I had gone into the woods or along the beach, I could always tell when Great-aunt Simone had arrived and was preparing her famous soup …

Preparation: 10 minutes
Cooking: 2 hours

Serves 6

4 tbsp olive oil
5 whole garlic bulbs, cut in half crossways
25g flour
1.5 litres hot water
4 sprigs of thyme
sea salt
freshly ground black pepper
100g thin vermicelli
a large bunch of flat-leaf parsley, finely chopped

Heat the oven to 140°C/gas 1.

Drizzle the oil over a roasting tray and put the cut garlic bulbs on it. Roast for 1–1½ hours, until soft and golden.

Remove the garlic from the oven and, when cool enough to handle, squeeze out the soft, buttery flesh. Put it in a saucepan with the juices from the roasting tray and mash with a spoon. Over a medium heat, mix in the flour so it absorbs the oil and makes a roux. Slowly pour in the hot water, stirring constantly. Add the thyme and seasoning and simmer for 20 minutes.

Remove from the heat, discard the thyme sprigs and use a hand-held blender to make the soup smooth. Return to the heat, add the vermicelli and cook for 3 minutes. Add parsley just before serving.

Watercress Soup

Potage au Cresson is a lovely fresh, green soup, perfect for summer. It's also a great excuse to go out and buy those enormous bundles of watercress you find on French markets.

Preparation: 20 minutes
Cooking: 40 minutes

Serves 6

2 tbsp olive oil
1 small onion, chopped
600g potatoes, diced
300g watercress, chopped
100ml water
1 litre chicken or vegetable stock
sea salt
freshly ground black pepper
a pinch of freshly grated nutmeg

Heat the olive oil in a saucepan and cook the onion and potato over a medium-low heat for 20 minutes. Add the watercress (keep a little back to use for garnish) and water and cook for 5 minutes until the watercress wilts.

Add the stock, seasoning and nutmeg, bring to the boil and gently simmer for 15 minutes. Blend with a hand-held blender until smooth. Check the seasoning, scatter with the reserved watercress and serve at once.

This is an old-fashioned but versatile dish with as many variations as you can think of. Try it with *merguez* and a little couscous, or with smoked German sausage and sauerkraut to add a new twist.

Sausage and Bean Winter Soup

Potage Haricots-Saucisses —the perfect comfort food for a miserable winter night.

Preparation: 30 minutes, plus overnight soaking
Cooking: 1 hour 45 minutes

Serves 6

200g dried white haricot beans
2 tbsp olive oil
100g thick-cut bacon, cubed
2 onions, finely diced
2 cloves of garlic, crushed, peeled and chopped
2 carrots, finely diced
2 sticks of celery, finely diced
1 litre chicken stock
1 bay leaf
sea salt
freshly ground black pepper
3 spicy Toulouse sausages (about 350–400g)
a bunch of flat-leaf parsley, chopped

Soak the beans overnight in a saucepan of cold water. The next day, drain them, rinse well and return to the pan. Cover with water, bring to the boil and simmer for 1 hour. Skim off any froth that rises to the top during cooking. Drain and set aside.

Heat the oil in a large saucepan and cook the bacon for 5 minutes until golden. Add the onions, garlic, carrot and celery, and gently sauté for 5 minutes. Pour in the stock, add the bay leaf and seasoning, and stir. Add the sausages whole and simmer for 25 minutes with a lid on the pan.

Add the drained haricot beans and simmer for a further 10 minutes. Remove the sausages, slice them and return the slices to the pan. Sprinkle the soup with chopped parsley and serve.

There is only one way to chop garlic. Place the unpeeled clove on a chopping board. Take a large knife and, using the flat of the blade under the heel of your hand, ruthlessly crush the garlic. Now you can easily peel it, chop it (as finely as you like) and put it in the pot.

You can still buy *galettes* from street vendors in most parts of Brittany, or you can make your own at home. They are good with *merguez* (red-looking, very spicy sausage made from beef, mutton and red pepper), cheese, ham or egg – or even simply with fresh butter – but for a special occasion try these *Galettes Poireau-Fromage*.

Buckwheat Pancakes with Leek and Cheese Filling

Galettes de sarrazin, buckwheat pancakes, are the ultimate fast food. In my mother's home town of Vitré, there is a stall which sells *galettes-saucisse* every market day, and one of my greatest treats was to buy them for lunch. They never made it to the table, though; ideally they should be eaten hot, out of a paper cornet, on a street corner or park bench.

Preparation: 15 minutes, plus 2 hours' standing time for the batter
Cooking: 1 hour

Serves 6

For the pancakes:
125g buckwheat flour
125g flour
3 eggs
250ml milk (you can replace the milk with cider vinegar for a stronger and more authentic flavour)
250ml water
vegetable oil

For the filling:
2 tbsp olive oil
2 cloves of garlic, crushed, peeled and chopped
200g thick-cut bacon, cubed
5 large leeks, sliced
sea salt
freshly ground black pepper
125g Tomme or other hard cheese
3 tbsp crème fraiche

First make the batter. Put the flours in large bowl, make a well in the centre, add the eggs, milk and water and beat together until smooth. Allow to stand for 2 hours before cooking.

Heat a non-stick frying or crêpe pan and wipe very lightly with vegetable oil. Ladle in just enough mixture to cover the bottom of the pan – tip the pan to make the mixture travel and coat the base evenly but lightly. Allow to set over a medium heat, then flip with a palette knife. Cook for a further minute and then turn out. Repeat until all the batter is used. You should end up with about 18 pancakes, even if you have had to throw the first one away. You can stack them up with baking parchment between the layers.

To make the filling, heat the oil in a pan over a medium heat, add the garlic, bacon and leeks, and cook for 10 minutes, stirring constantly. The aim is to cook the leeks until they are soft and any excess liquid has evaporated. Add the seasoning. Remove from the heat and stir in the grated cheese and crème fraiche.

Place a spoonful of mixture on each pancake and fold into quarters to make little triangular cones. Serve at once.

Cheese Fondue

Serve luxuriously rich and creamy *Fondue Franc-Comtoise* with a crisp green salad to clear the palate.

Preparation: 15 minutes
Cooking: 15 minutes

Serves 6

1 clove of garlic, crushed and peeled
800g Gruyère de Savoie or Beaufort cheese, grated
1 tbsp cornflour
300ml white wine
freshly ground black pepper
2 large baguettes, cut into cubes

Rub the inside of a thick-based pan with the crushed garlic clove. Mix the cheese and cornflour in a bowl.

Pour the wine into the garlic-scented pan and heat to boiling. Reduce the heat to low and add handfuls of the cheese, stirring until all the cheese is melted. Season with pepper. Serve the fondue at once, with cubes of bread for dipping.

Blue Cheese Bake

The French name for this dish – *Soupe au Fromage* – is wonderfully misleading. It isn't a soup by modern standards, but it is an old and very comforting baked cheese dish from the Auvergne region. It's very good as a main course, too, with a crisp green salad on the side.

Preparation: 30 minutes
Cooking: 15 minutes

Serves 6

olive oil
4 red onions, diced
2 cloves of garlic, crushed, peeled and chopped
200ml dry white wine
200ml chicken or vegetable stock
12 slices country-style bread (about 600g)
6 tomatoes, peeled
a bunch of basil
300g St Agur, Roquefort or other blue cheese, sliced or crumbled
sea salt
freshly ground black pepper

Heat the oven to 200°C/gas 6.

Heat a little oil in a pan and gently sauté the onions and garlic for 10 minutes until soft – do not brown or frizzle them. Add the white wine and stock, gently bring to a simmer, then remove from the heat.

Toast the slices of bread. Slice the tomatoes and roughly tear the basil. Rub a shallow ovenproof dish with a little olive oil. Cover the base with a layer of toasted bread topped with sliced tomato, basil, cheese and seasoning. Repeat until all the ingredients are used except for 100g cheese. Pour the onion and wine over the bread and top with the remaining cheese. Bake for 15 minutes, then serve at once.

Pissaladière

I love the strong flavours of this dish, which combines two of my personal addictions: anchovies and olives. Use the best olives you can find – in the south of France there are olive markets which sell hundreds of differently spiced varieties – and those fat brown anchovies preserved in salt rather than oil.

Preparation: 1 hour, plus 1½ hours' proving
Cooking: 1 hour 30 minutes

Serves 6

6 tbsp olive oil, plus extra for brushing
25g butter
a bunch of thyme
1.75kg onions, very finely sliced (quickest done on a mandolin cutter)
sea salt
freshly ground black pepper
15g dried yeast
120ml tepid water
1 tsp unrefined sugar
250g strong flour
sea salt
12 anchovies
black olives, pitted

Warm 2 tablespoons of the olive oil and melt the butter in a large saucepan over a low heat. Strip the thyme leaves from the stalks and add about half to the pan. Add the onions – it is important that the onions are very finely sliced – and cook over a low heat for 1 hour, stirring occasionally: they should be soft and slightly caramelized but not brown. Season and leave to cool.

Mix the yeast with the tepid water and sugar. Leave for 10 minutes in a warm place until the mixture becomes frothy.

Put the flour and a little salt in a mixing bowl, add the yeast mixture and 4 tablespoons of the olive oil, and mix until you have a dough ball. Lightly flour a work surface and knead the dough for 10 minutes until the mixture is smooth and soft. Brush the inside of a bowl with a little olive oil, put the dough in and cover with a cloth. Leave in a warm place to prove until the dough has doubled in size, which takes about 1 hour.

Brush a baking sheet with a little olive oil.

Knock the air out of the dough on a lightly floured surface and knead for 2 minutes. Roll the dough out to 30cm x 25cm, place on the baking sheet and brush the surface of the dough with a little more olive oil. Cover with the cooked onions. Slice each anchovy into four long ribbons and arrange on top of the onions in a lattice pattern. Place the olives between the criss-crossed anchovies and sprinkle with the remaining thyme. Leave somewhere warm to prove again for 30 minutes.

Heat the oven to 220°C/gas 7.

Bake the pissaladière for 20–25 minutes, and serve warm.

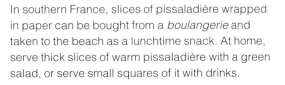

In southern France, slices of pissaladière wrapped in paper can be bought from a *boulangerie* and taken to the beach as a lunchtime snack. At home, serve thick slices of warm pissaladière with a green salad, or serve small squares of it with drinks.

The tastes in *Tarte Paysanne* vary according to the tomatoes you use. Ideally, use fresh, ripe, locally grown ones for the best flavour. Small, part-roasted cherry tomatoes work quite well, but my favourites are the big, shapeless *Marmande* tomatoes you can buy on French markets and which taste so good you might just want to eat them on their own …

Roast Tomato Tart

Tarte Paysanne has a rich, sunny flavour. Make it with the best tomatoes you can find.

Preparation: 40 minutes, plus chilling
Cooking: 40 minutes

Serves 6

For the pastry:
200g flour
75g butter, cut into small pieces
25g lard, cut into small pieces
1 egg, beaten

For the filling:
3 tbsp thick double cream or crème fraiche
3 tbsp Dijon mustard
10–12 large tomatoes, cored, peeled and sliced
sea salt
freshly ground black pepper
4 sprigs of fresh thyme
olive oil for drizzling

To make the pastry, put the flour in a bowl, add the butter and lard, and rub together with your fingertips until the mixture resembles breadcrumbs. Using a round-bladed knife in a cutting motion, combine the egg with the mix until a pastry ball forms. Turn out on a lightly floured surface and quickly knead until even and smooth, then wrap and chill for 30 minutes.
    Heat the oven to 190°C/gas 5.
    Roll out the pastry and line a 30cm push-up-bottom tart case. Mix together the cream and Dijon mustard and spread over the pastry base. Arrange the sliced tomatoes in the case, season, and scatter thyme leaves – stripped from the stalks – over the top. Bake for 40 minutes. Drizzle with a little olive oil and serve warm or cold.

Quiche Lorraine

This is the original quiche, and once you have tasted the home-made variety you will never want to buy another one again. It is best served just warm (not hot), to bring out the creaminess of the filling and the contrast of textures.

Preparation: 40 minutes, plus chilling
Cooking: 50 minutes

Serves 6

For the pastry:
250g flour
70g butter, cut into small pieces
55g lard, cut into small pieces
2 egg yolks, lightly beaten with 2 tbsp cold water

For the filling:
olive oil
300g thick-cut smoked bacon, cubed
2 eggs
100ml double cream
sea salt
freshly ground black pepper

To make the pastry, put the flour in a bowl, add the butter and lard, and rub together with your fingertips until the mixture resembles breadcrumbs. Using a round-bladed knife in a cutting motion, combine the beaten egg yolks with the mix until a pastry ball forms. Turn out on a lightly floured surface and quickly knead until the pastry is even and smooth, then wrap and chill for 30 minutes.
    Heat the oven to 180°C/gas 4.
    Roll out the pastry and line a 30cm push-up-bottom flan tin. Heat a little olive oil in a frying pan and cook the bacon for 5 minutes. In a bowl, beat the eggs, cream and seasoning until blended, then add the bacon. Pour into the pastry case. Bake for 35 minutes, reduce the temperature to 160°C/gas 3, and bake for a further 15 minutes. Serve warm.

Peeled tomatoes take on a whole, new velvety texture. Once you start peeling tomatoes for your recipes, you won't look back. Make a cross in the bottom of each one, plunge into boiling water for 10 seconds (a little more if the tomatoes are not fully ripe), remove and peel. It's that simple.

Onion Tart

Beautifully smoky-sweet and delicate, *Tarte à l'Oignon* is perfect as a main course with a summer salad, or as an autumn starter.

Preparation: 40 minutes, plus chilling
Cooking: 1 hour 15 minutes

Serves 6

For the pastry:
250g flour
175g butter, cut into small pieces
2 egg yolks, lightly beaten
beans for baking blind

For the filling:
50g butter
2 tbsp olive oil
400g onions, finely sliced (use a mandolin for the quickest and best result)
120ml single cream
2 eggs
1/2 tsp freshly grated nutmeg
sea salt
freshly ground black pepper

To make the pastry, put the flour in a bowl, add the butter, and rub together with your fingertips until the mixture resembles breadcrumbs. Using a round-bladed knife in a cutting motion, combine the egg yolks with the mix until a pastry ball forms. Turn out on a lightly floured surface and quickly knead until the pastry is even and smooth, then wrap and place in the fridge to chill for 30 minutes.
    Heat the oven to 200°C/gas 6.

Roll out the pastry on a lightly floured surface and line a 30cm push-up-bottom flan tin, making sure there are no cracks. Return to the fridge to chill for another 20 minutes, then line with baking parchment and fill with baking beans. Bake for 20 minutes, reduce the heat to 160°C/gas 3, and cook for a further 15 minutes, or until the pastry is golden and set.
    While the pastry is baking, make the filling. Melt the butter with the oil in a saucepan. Add the finely sliced onions and cook over a low heat for 30 minutes. This long, slow method of cooking makes the onions melt; do not allow them to brown or frizzle.
    Mix the cream, eggs, nutmeg and seasoning in a bowl. Put the cooked onions in the baked pastry case, carefully pour in the egg mixture and then return the tart to the oven to cook for 25–30 minutes. Serve warm or cold.

Tartelette Méridionale

A terrific summer dish, lush with the flavours of southern France, as its name suggests …

Preparation: 30 minutes
Cooking: 1 hour 50 minutes

Serves 6

For the pastry:
200g flour
75g butter, cut into small pieces
25g lard, cut into small pieces
1 egg, beaten
beans for baking blind

For the filling:
olive oil
50 cherry tomatoes, halved
1 clove of garlic, crushed, peeled and chopped
100g tapenade, bought or home-made
6 anchovy fillets
a bunch of fresh basil
100g olives, pitted
sea salt
freshly ground black pepper

To make the pastry, put the flour in a bowl, add the butter and lard, and rub together with your fingertips until the mixture resembles breadcrumbs. Using a round-bladed knife in a cutting motion, combine the egg with the mix until a pastry ball forms. Turn out on a lightly floured surface and quickly knead until the pastry is even and smooth, then wrap and place in the fridge to chill for 30 minutes.

Heat the oven to 180°C/gas 4.

Roll out the pastry on a lightly floured surface and line six 10cm push-up-bottom tart tins. Line each tart tin with baking parchment, cover with a layer of baking beans and bake for 25 minutes. Take out of the oven, remove the

beans and baking parchment, and set the cases aside. Reduce the temperature to 120°C/gas 1/2.

Pour a little oil in a roasting tin, add the tomatoes and garlic and toss well. Roast in the low-temperature oven for 1 hour.

Roughly spread about a teaspoon of the tapenade over the base of each pastry case. Top with 1 anchovy fillet, a few basil leaves, the roasted tomatoes and a few olives. Drizzle with olive oil – you could use what's left in the roasting tin – season, and cook for a further 10 minutes.

Tapenade

This is what I eat when I've had too much chocolate. It's lovely to make by hand with a pestle and mortar, which really brings out the scents of the ingredients. It's versatile, too; you can serve it with good bread, as a dip with crudités or tossed over warm pasta, and if you add a little extra oil to the mixture, it makes an excellent dressing for celery or lettuce hearts. You can make tapenade in advance and it will last in the fridge for up to 4 days (if you can resist it!). Add chilli for a change if you like, and see my note about anchovies on page 23.

Preparation: 20 minutes

Serves 6

300g pitted black or green olives
8 anchovy fillets
3 tbsp capers, rinsed of their salt
1 clove of garlic
juice of 1/2 lemon
sea salt and freshly ground black pepper
180ml extra-virgin olive oil

Put all the ingredients except the oil in a mortar or a blender and pound or blend to a rough chop. Slowly pour in the olive oil and combine to form a paste. Store in the fridge.

Chilli Garlic Bread is my daughter's favourite recipe: she loves both the making and the eating of it. It's easy enough for her to prepare without too much help while at the same time allowing her to create plenty of enjoyable mess.

Anouchka's Chilli Garlic Bread

My daughter's favourite recipe. If the strength of the garlic seems a little overpowering to you, roast it in the oven for a sweeter, more delicate taste before blending it in with the other ingredients in a pestle and mortar. Don't use a blender – half the fun of this very simple recipe is mixing it by hand and getting messy! Do take care, though, with little people's eyes and skin or it could all end in tears: make sure children wash their hands after touching the chilli.

Preparation: 10 minutes
Cooking: 10 minutes

Serves 6

1 medium-hot red chilli
4 cloves of garlic, crushed, peeled and chopped
a sprig of thyme
1 tsp coarse sea salt
175g butter, soft
1 baguette

Heat the oven to 180°C/gas 4.

Cut the chilli in half lengthways, remove the seeds and dice the flesh. (Keep the seeds in if you like the heat.) Put the chilli, garlic, thyme leaves (stripped from the stalks) and salt in a pestle and mortar, and pound until it forms a paste. Put the butter in a bowl, add the paste and mix well.

Almost-slice the bread to the bottom every 3cm and then divide the butter mix among each incision, spreading it over the inner surfaces. Put the bread on a baking tray and bake for 8–10 minutes. Eat at once.

Joe's Potato Bread

This is not a true bread as we are used to it. It is denser, because of the potato, and contains no yeast. It will rise only marginally: don't expect miracles. But it makes a dense and comforting bread, perfect with soup on a chilly winter's day.

Preparation: 2 hours, including proving
Cooking: 40 minutes

Serves 6

350g floury potatoes, washed
a bunch of flat-leaf parsley, chopped
90g butter, melted
2 egg yolks
300g self-raising flour
50g raisins
20g sunflower seeds
2 tbsp milk
sea salt
1 egg

Heat the oven to 200°C/gas 6.

Pierce the potatoes with a knife several times and bake for 40 minutes until soft inside. Set the potatoes aside until cool enough to handle, then cut them in half and scoop the flesh out into a bowl. Mash it and set aside to cool.

Add the parsley, butter and egg yolks to the cooled potato, and blend well. Then add the flour, raisins, sunflower seeds, milk and salt, and mix well again until it forms a dough ball.

Lightly flour a surface and knead the dough for 5 minutes until the mixture is smooth. Cover and leave in a warm place for 35 minutes to prove and rise a little.

Heat the oven to 180°C/gas 4.

Knead the bread again for 5 minutes. Butter a loaf tin, shape the bread to fit the tin and leave to rise for 35 minutes in a warm place.

Beat the egg and brush the top of the bread all over, then bake it for 40 minutes. Serve warm, and eat on the same day as baking.

Three-mushroom Vol-au-vents

Vol-au-vent means 'blown on the wind', and these little pastries should be almost as light as air.

Preparation: 2 hours
Cooking: 45 minutes

Serves 6

For the puff pastry:
200g flour
25g lard, cut into small pieces
175g butter, cut into small pieces
150ml icy water
1 beaten egg for glazing

For the filling:
1 tbsp olive oil
200g girolles, roughly chopped
200g chanterelles, roughly chopped
200g button mushrooms, roughly chopped
2 shallots, diced
100ml double cream
1 tbsp grainy mustard (such as Meaux)
1 tbsp cognac
sea salt
freshly ground black pepper

To make the pastry, put the flour in a bowl, add the lard and 25g of the butter (cut it into pieces first) and rub together with your fingertips until the mixture resembles breadcrumbs. Add the icy water, mixing it in with a round-bladed knife until a ball forms. Turn out on a lightly floured surface and quickly knead the pastry until even and smooth, then wrap and chill for 30 minutes.

Lightly dust a cool work surface with flour and roll the pastry out to approximately 12cm x 25cm. Cut the remaining butter into small pieces and dot over the rolled-out pastry. Fold a third of the pastry over towards the centre, then fold the remaining single layer over to make 3 layers. Press the edges together to stop the butter escaping.

Turn it 90 degrees, lightly dust and roll out once more to the above size. Again, turn the pastry 90 degrees, fold 3 times and press the edges together. Roll out and repeat one more time. Wrap and place in the fridge to chill and relax for 30 minutes. Remove and repeat the above process before chilling for another 30 minutes. Then repeat the whole process one more time. (You could buy prepared vol-au-vent cases, but this is more fun, and the result is better.)

Heat the oven to 220°C/gas 7.

Roll out the pastry to 5mm thickness and cut out 12 small or 6 large rounds with a pastry cutter. Place them on a damp baking sheet and return to the fridge to chill for 30 minutes. Take a cutter half the size of your first one and make indentations in the centre of each pastry circle, being careful not to cut all the way through to the baking sheet. Take a small knife and knock up all around the edges of the vol-au-vent cases to help the pastry to rise in crispy layers.

Brush the top of each case with the beaten egg, making sure no egg goes down the sides where it will glue the layers together and undo the effect of your knocking up. Bake for 30 minutes. While the cases are baking, make the filling.

Heat the olive oil in a large frying pan, add the mushrooms and shallots, and cook over a medium-high heat, stirring constantly. If there are a lot of juices in the pan, increase the heat and cook until they reduce. Remove 6 mushrooms for garnish, and keep them warm. Add the cream, mustard, cognac and seasoning, and simmer for 5 minutes, stirring constantly.

After the pastry cases have been in the oven for 30 minutes, take them out and lift out the centre of each pastry case, putting it to one side. Return the tray to the oven and cook for 3 more minutes, then fill with the mushroom mixture, top with the reserved mushrooms and the pastry caps, and serve.

Even children who won't eat cabbage should enjoy this tasty, hearty dish. As a child it took me a long time to realize that this firm, delicious green leaf and the anaemic white stuff I was given at school were one and the same ingredient …

Cabbage Galette

This is an old peasant dish from the Auvergne region, and although it is known as *Galette au Chou*, it is quite different from the thin Breton *galettes*. It is dense and filling, and can be eaten hot or cold, although I think this dish is best served just warm.

Preparation: 20 minutes
Cooking: 30 minutes

Serves 6

1/2 Savoy cabbage, roughly chopped
2 tbsp olive oil
200g thick-cut smoked bacon, cubed
2 eggs
3 shallots, finely diced
3 cloves of garlic, crushed, peeled and chopped
a bunch of flat-leaf parsley, finely chopped
sea salt
freshly ground black pepper
200g flour
250ml milk

Heat the oven to 180°C/gas 4.
    Steam the cabbage for 3 minutes. Smear a pie dish with olive oil and heat in the oven.
    In a bowl, mix together the bacon, eggs, shallots, garlic, parsley and seasoning. Add the flour and milk and blend into a smooth dough.
    Remove the hot pie dish from the oven. Spread half the dough over the base of the dish, pile on the cabbage and pack it down with your hands, and cover with the remaining dough. Bake for 35 minutes until golden and firm.

Fish

My favourite fish recipe begins like this:
Take a boat, a fishing rod, a frying pan and a jar of mustard … Many people avoid cooking fish because they think it will be difficult, but fish recipes can be as easy or as complicated as you want to make them. The essential thing is that your fish should be absolutely fresh. During my childhood I spent my holidays near my uncle Paul, who was a fisherman, and there was always a plentiful supply of freshly caught local fish. This

is the ideal situation, but failing that, it's a good idea to befriend an approachable fishmonger who can advise you and who will prepare your fish for you on the spot (ready-filleted fish loses its taste rapidly). All along the French coast you can find terrific fish markets, and in many harbours you can buy fresh-caught shellfish, crabs and lobsters from the fishermen themselves. It is wonderful holiday food, because most fish and shellfish are very quick and simple to prepare and to cook, even on a portable stove or barbecue.

Don't be nervous of using mussels, cockles, clams and other shellfish. Just make sure they are very fresh – if you buy them from a fish shop, make sure it's a busy one with a fast turnover. The shells should be closed. Sometimes the low temperature of the fridge acts as an anaesthetic and the shells open: just bang them on a hard surface and slowly they should shut, and if not, discard them. Wash them well in a large sink of cold running water. Use a small knife to rip away the stringy beard around the lip. Discard any damaged shells, and any shells that do not open when cooked.

One of the great pleasures of the French coast is going into a café and ordering fresh seafood and one of the dry, cheerful local wines. Muscadet or Gros-Plant makes an excellent accompaniment, though a rosé (such as an Anjou) gives a more fragrant, flowery taste. Serve very cold.

MOULES
de BOUCHOT

2,50 €
Le litre

Moules Marinière

I first tasted this dish when I was six years old. Like many small children, I was reluctant to eat shellfish at first, but on this occasion my mother persuaded me to taste hers. Unfortunately for my mother, I not only tasted her dish, but finished the lot, and I have loved mussels ever since. On Noirmoutier I used to collect them from the rocks in front of the house, pick the bay leaves off the tree in the next-door neighbour's garden, dig for the garlic in the dunes, where it grew wild, and cook the whole lot in sea water, which my mother insists is the key ingredient. Serve with warm crusty bread and a green salad.

Preparation: 20 minutes
Cooking: 15 minutes

Serves 6

50g butter
2 tbsp olive oil
2 cloves of garlic, crushed, peeled and finely diced
1 onion, finely diced
1.5kg mussels, cleaned and washed (see page 68)
200ml white wine (Muscadet works well)
a bay leaf
sea salt
freshly ground black pepper
large bunch of flat-leaf parsley, chopped

Gently heat the butter and olive oil in a large saucepan, add the garlic and onion and sauté for 5 minutes – do not brown or frizzle them. Then add the mussels, wine, bay leaf and seasoning, bring to the boil, cover and cook for 10 minutes, or until all the mussel shells have opened. Finally, add the parsley, put the lid back on and shake vigorously. Serve at once.

Georges Payen's Razor Clams

This is a quick and delicious way of serving razor clams – *couteaux* – with garlic and chilli, perfect for a warm summer night on the beach. At my grandfather's house you could catch the clams – if you were very patient and quiet – when the tide was out, and finding and catching these shellfish was one of my favourite pastimes as a child, although it took me a long time to enjoy eating the clams themselves! These elusive creatures live deep in the sand and come out only when the tide is high. You have to sprinkle salt around the clam's hole to fool it into believing the tide has come in, then, when it pops out – only for a split second – you have to grab it very fast, or it disappears again for good. In those days before computer games, it was a great exercise in hand-eye co-ordination. Now, of course, you can buy clams from the fishmonger, which is less time-consuming (but much less fun). Serve with lots of warm bread to mop up the cooking juices.

Preparation: 10 minutes
Cooking: 10 minutes

Serves 6

a dash of olive oil
25g butter
24 razor clams
2 cloves of garlic, crushed, peeled and finely diced
1 red chilli, halved, deseeded and finely diced
100ml white wine
a bunch of flat-leaf parsley, chopped
freshly ground black pepper

Heat the olive oil and butter in a large pan, add the razor clams, garlic and chilli and cook for 5 minutes. Pour in the white wine, place a lid on the pan and cook rapidly for a further 5 minutes. Finally, add the parsley and pepper, toss and serve at once.

Noirmoutier Oysters

Some recipes use cooked oysters, but much more usual is to eat them raw, with nothing but a little lemon juice or shallot vinegar, a glass of Muscadet and a view of the ocean.

Preparation: 30 minutes

Serves 6

2 shallots, peeled and very finely diced
3 tbsp red wine vinegar
24 Brittany or Vendée oysters
seaweed or crushed ice, to garnish
1 lemon, cut into wedges
sourdough bread, finely sliced
Tabasco
freshly ground black pepper

Mix the shallots and vinegar together in a small bowl. Shuck the oysters: place each oyster, rounded side down, in a cloth and hold with one hand. Insert an oyster knife at the narrow end of the oyster, between the two shells, and wiggle, keeping the blade flat. You may need some strength, but the shell will eventually give and open. Run the knife along the inside of the top shell to release the oyster muscle, remove the top shell and cut the oyster free from the bottom shell.

Arrange the prepared oysters on a bed of crushed ice or seaweed. Serve with the shallot vinegar, lemon wedges, sourdough bread, the bottle of Tabasco and the pepper mill at the table.

The coast of Brittany and the Vendée is traditionally oyster (*huître*) country. Cancale oysters are particularly good, but you can find oysters all the way down the coast.

Seafood Platter

If I were to plan my last meal, *Fruits de Mer* would be the main course. To me it evokes everything that is good about food: the joy of excellent ingredients, simply presented; the time it takes to eat, and the pleasure of eating in an informal environment, surrounded by friends and family. This is not a dish to be consumed in haste, or in silence, or in pretentious or intimidating surroundings, or in uncongenial company. It requires time and leisure. It encourages conversation, co-operation, intimacy and friendship. It is the ideal thing for a large and cheery get-together – and even better for a candlelit dinner for two, with lots of chilled champagne.

Preparation: 30 minutes
Cooking: 35 minutes

Serves 6

$^1/_2$ litre large clams
12 langoustines
3 crabs
500g prawns (size according to budget!)
1 litre mussels
$^1/_2$ litre whelks
$^1/_2$ litre winkles
seaweed or crushed ice, to serve
12 Brittany oysters
3 lemons, cut in half
red wine shallot vinegar (see the oyster recipe on page 72)
Tabasco
hearty, dense country bread, thinly sliced

Reserve all your cooking water as you go, and freeze it for a fish stew or soup. Here goes.

Clams: purge them by soaking them in a large bowl of water and then draining and repeating the soaking until no more sand comes out of them. Open as for oysters (see page 72).

Langoustines: plunge them into a pan of boiling water and simmer for 5 minutes, then drain and chill them.

Crabs: plunge them into a pan of boiling water and simmer for 6 minutes per 500g, then drain and chill them. Separate the central part of the underbody from the shell with your hands or a knife. Remove and discard the soft grey-coloured, feather-like gills.

Prawns: plunge them into a pan of boiling water and simmer for 3–5 minutes. Drain and chill them.

Mussels: heat a scant amount of water in a pan with a little knob of butter, add the cleaned mussels (see page 68), place the lid on and simmer for 5 minutes.

Whelks: plunge them into a pan of boiling water and simmer for 10 minutes, then drain and chill them.

Winkles: plunge them into a pan of boiling water and simmer for 5 minutes, then drain and chill them.

To serve, cover a huge platter with seaweed or crushed ice. Open the oysters with an oyster knife (see page 72) and place them together on the platter. Using the oyster knife, open the clams and cluster them together. Arrange the langoustines, prawns, whelks and winkles all together. Place the mussels in a bowl on the platter. Crown the seafood with the cooked crabs and then garnish with lemon halves. Serve with a dish of shallot vinegar, a bottle of Tabasco and a basket of slices of bread. Eat at once with finger bowls and large napkins on the side.

Jean Sorin's Fisherman's Stew

Soupe du Pêcheur is an extrovert, sociable dish, impossible to eat without a certain amount of mess. It is excellent comfort food for the evening after a long, cold day's fishing, with a loaf of really good country bread.

Preparation: 15 minutes
Cooking: 40 minutes

Serves 6

3 tbsp olive oil
3 onions, chopped
3 cloves of garlic, crushed, peeled and chopped
2 red chillies, halved, deseeded and chopped
a pinch of saffron
sea salt
freshly ground black pepper
2 x 410g tins chopped tomatoes
1 tbsp tomato purée
300ml white wine
600g new potatoes
500g mixed, cleaned shellfish: mussels, prawns, scallops or clams
1kg fish fillets: try any combination of red mullet, John Dory, halibut, bream, bass, haddock, tuna, swordfish and/or marlin
a large bunch of flat-leaf parsley, finely chopped

Heat the olive oil in a large pan. Add the onions, garlic, chilli, saffron and seasoning and soften over a gentle heat for 10 minutes. Add the chopped tomatoes, purée and white wine. Bring to the boil and simmer for 5 minutes to reduce some of the liquid.

Add the potatoes and simmer gently for 15 minutes.

Add the cleaned shellfish and then carefully lay the fish fillets on top. Cover with a lid and simmer for a further 10 minutes.

Just before serving, add lots of chopped parsley. Serve in large open soup bowls, with plenty of finger bowls at the table.

My great-uncle Jean taught me this dish – but it is best not to rely entirely on one's own fishing to provide all the ingredients. I always allow for a visit to the local fish market before I begin …

Rich Bouillabaisse

This very old recipe was originally cooked in a pot balanced on three stones, and was a poor dish designed to make the most of cheap, common ingredients. It is almost impossible to make authentic bouillabaisse other than in the south of France, because the rascasse and other Mediterranean rock fish that are traditionally used in its making are just not available elsewhere. This 'rich' version – *Bouillabaisse Riche* – uses monkfish instead, which has fewer bones, but you can adapt the recipe to any kind of fish or shellfish. In Marseille, the *bouillon* is served with a local bread called *marette*, with the fish on the side, and the legend goes that the goddess Venus first made it for her husband Vulcan – to send him to sleep while she disported herself elsewhere. Serve bouillabaisse with lots of warm French bread, and try it with a spoonful of chilli aïoli, a variation of the herb aïoli on page 29.

Preparation: 30 minutes
Cooking: 35 minutes

Serves 6

4 tbsp olive oil
2 cloves of garlic, crushed, peeled and diced
2 onions, diced
2 leeks, trimmed and finely sliced
3 sticks of celery, finely sliced
1 bulb of fennel, trimmed and diced
1 tbsp flour
2 bay leaves
a sprig of thyme
a pinch of saffron
2 x 410g tins chopped tomatoes
1 litre fish stock
600g monkfish, trimmed and cut into 6 portions
6 scallops, cleaned
6 large raw prawns
sea salt
freshly ground black pepper
a good bunch of chives, finely chopped

Heat the olive oil in a large saucepan. Add the garlic, onions, leeks, celery and fennel, and sauté over a medium heat for 10 minutes, stirring frequently – do not allow them to brown.

Sprinkle in the flour and blend it in to absorb any excess oil, then add the bay leaves, thyme, saffron and tomatoes and mix well. Pour in the fish stock, bring to the boil, then reduce the heat and simmer for 15 minutes.

Add the monkfish, scallops, prawns and seasoning, cover with a lid, and simmer very gently for 10 minutes.

Just before serving, add the chives. Serve the bouillabaisse in large soup bowls.

Salmon in a Parcel

This is an excellent way to cook fish so that it stays tender and moist, with a light, delicate flavour. Its French name is *Saumon en Papillote*.

Preparation: 40 minutes
Cooking: 15 minutes

Serves 6

5 sticks of celery, sliced
4 shallots, sliced
a bunch of flat-leaf parsley, chopped
sea salt
freshly ground black pepper
6 x 150g salmon fillets, skinless
1 lemon, cut into 6 wedges

Heat the oven to 200°C/gas 6. Cut six 25cm circles out of baking parchment.

Put the celery and shallots in a bowl, add the parsley and the seasoning and mix well.

Arrange the paper circles over the work surface. Place a spoonful of the vegetable mixture in the middle of each paper and top with a salmon fillet and a wedge of lemon. Close up each parcel, securing the contents by twisting the paper above the fish like an old-fashioned purse. Place on a baking tray and bake for 15 minutes. Serve in the paper parcels, but take care when opening as hot steam may rush out.

Salmon in Red Wine

This unusual combination – *Saumon au Vin Rouge* – makes for a rich, earthy dish, excellent with pasta (serve it for example on piles of ribbon pasta) or rice.

Preparation: 10 minutes
Cooking: 20 minutes

Serves 6

50g butter
1 tbsp olive oil
1 red onion, chopped
1 clove of garlic, crushed, peeled and chopped
100g mushrooms, sliced
30g flour
1 bottle red Burgundy
freshly ground black pepper
sea salt
6 x 150g salmon fillets (skin left on)

Melt the butter with the olive oil in a big, wide saucepan, add the onion, garlic and mushrooms and sauté gently for 10 minutes.

Sprinkle in the flour and mix well until it has absorbed the oil and butter, then gradually add the red wine and mix until smooth. Season. Bring to the boil. Add the salmon fillets to the pan and spoon the red wine over them to stain them evenly. Cover, then simmer gently for 8 minutes.

Lift out the salmon and keep it warm. Bring the wine back to the boil, mix well, then with a slotted spoon lift out all the mushrooms and serve them with the salmon.

Don't discard the wine – it can be stored in the freezer and re-used.

BAR BEL

KARAOKE AU SO

SERVICE
RAPIDE
&
AU BAR

SPECIALIT
DE BIERE

DEGUSTEZ
NOS VIANDES
ROTIES
A LA BROCHE

Rochefortoise

A light, fresh dish for a summer by the sea, this Breton recipe, *Raie aux Câpres*, makes the most of the delicate consistency of the skate, the tangy capers an ideal contrast to the fish's rather sweet flesh.

84

Skate with Herb Butter

This is delicious with Nutmeg Mash, page 167.
Use salt-preserved anchovies, if you can.

Preparation: 20 minutes
Cooking: 15 minutes

Serves 6

a bunch of watercress
a bunch of flat-leaf parsley
a bunch of chervil
a bunch of tarragon
a bunch of chives
1 clove of garlic
25g capers
3 anchovy fillets
250g butter, softened
juice of 1/2 lemon
freshly ground black pepper
6 x 150g portions of skate wing

Heat the oven to 200°C/gas 6.

Trim the stems of the watercress and herbs then put the leaves into a small blender with the garlic, capers and anchovies and whiz until finely chopped. (You could do this by hand, but you would need a little patience.) Add the butter, lemon juice and pepper and blend until evenly mixed. Scoop out and place in a serving bowl.

Heat a large, lightly oiled roasting tray in the oven for 5 minutes.

Pat the skate wings dry with kitchen paper to remove excess moisture, then lay them on the heated roasting tray. Drizzle with a little olive oil and roast in the top of the oven for 15 minutes. Serve immediately with scoops of the soft herb butter.

Trout with Fennel

Fennel gives a spicy aniseed flavour to this rich and creamy dish: *Truite au Fenouil*.

Preparation: 25 minutes
Cooking: 45 minutes

Serves 6

6 trout, gutted and cleaned (ask your fishmonger)
olive oil
3 bulbs of fennel, trimmed, cored and finely sliced
200g Parmesan, grated
sea salt
freshly ground black pepper
100ml double cream
100ml white wine

Heat the oven to 180°C/gas 4. Rinse the trout under cold water and dry with kitchen paper. Place on a large, lightly oiled baking tray.

Lightly oil a large baking dish and layer the fennel with half of the Parmesan, seasoning each layer. Pour the cream and white wine over the top, and sprinkle over the remaining Parmesan.

Cover the fennel dish with foil and bake for 20 minutes, then remove the foil and bake for a further 30 minutes. During the second baking, add the fish to the oven and bake these for 20 minutes.

Serve the trout on a bed of fennel.

Normandy Trout

Truite au Trou Normand is a simple dish that takes on another dimension when the flambéed Calvados is poured over just before serving.

Preparation: 10 minutes
Cooking: 20 minutes

Serves 6

6 trout, gutted and cleaned (ask your fishmonger)
100g butter
sea salt
freshly ground black pepper
100ml Calvados

Heat the oven to 140°C/gas 1.

Rinse the trout under cold water and dry with kitchen paper. Melt half of the butter over a medium heat in a large frying pan, add 3 trout, and cook on each side for 6 minutes.

Place in an ovenproof serving dish and keep warm in the oven while you melt the remaining butter and cook the other trout in the same way. Add them to the ones already in the serving dish and season.

Pour the Calvados into the frying pan over a high heat, allow it to ignite, pour it over the trout and serve at once.

Pike with Butter Sauce

The Loire is a long, murky and dangerous river, broad enough to have sandy islets along some parts of its length, and endlessly fascinating to children. It is there, with my friends Eric and Pilou Imbach, that I learned to build rafts out of river débris, to dive under the submerged tree-roots (swimming in the Loire was absolutely forbidden, which is why I did it), and to fish for pike. The fish were virtually inedible, half bones and half sewage, and my mother was obliged to find all kinds of ingenious ways of 'forgetting' our catch when it was time for me to go home. All the same, it was terrific fun, and has left me with a fondness for this fish.

Preparation: 20 minutes
Cooking: 1 hour

Serves 6

1 whole pike, approximately 2kg

For the *court bouillon*:
3 litres water
1 litre white wine
2 carrots, chopped
2 onions, chopped
2 sticks of celery, chopped
2 cloves of garlic, crushed, peeled and chopped
2 sprigs of thyme
2 bay leaves
a bunch of flat-leaf parsley
1 tbsp salt
5g black peppercorns
a pinch of fennel seeds

For the *beurre blanc*:
2 shallots, diced
200ml *court bouillon* stock
juice of 1/2 lemon
500g butter, softened
flat-leaf parsley to garnish

Place all the *court bouillon* ingredients in a large poaching pan or fish kettle, cover with a lid and bring to the boil, then simmer for 25 minutes.

Prepare the pike: gut and clean it well under running cold water, and cut off the fins and tail, and, if you must, the head. (You can always ask your fishmonger to do this.)

Carefully add the pike to the *court bouillon* in the fish kettle, bring to a very gentle simmer and cook for 30 minutes. Remove from the heat and allow the fish to rest in the *court bouillon* while you make the *beurre blanc*, after first taking 200ml of the liquid to use in it.

Simmer the shallots, *court bouillon* and lemon juice in a frying pan until reduced by half. Add small knobs of the butter and mix constantly with a balloon whisk over a medium heat until all the butter is absorbed and you have a creamy glossy sauce. Do not boil.

Lift the pike out of the fish kettle, drain and garnish with parsley. Serve the sauce separately.

Pike, properly cooked (and caught in less polluted waters than those in which I fished as a child), has a refined taste quite at variance with its troubling personal habits. This recipe, *Brochet au Beurre Blanc*, is one of the oldest and most traditional ways of cooking the 'bandit of the Loire'.

It's no surprise to learn that the pike is nicknamed
grand loup d'eau (great water wolf). Its large
mouth is filled with very sharp teeth, and many
people cut off the head before cooking. Order it
from your fishmonger, and ask for a river pike,
rather than a pond one, because the flesh is
white and cleaner. This is for a celebration meal.

Sole with Spinach

I love the simplicity of this recipe, *Sole aux Epinards*: the slight bitterness of the wilted greens contrasts with the melting sweetness of the sole and the creamy shallot sauce.

Preparation: 20 minutes
Cooking: 20 minutes

Serves 6

125g butter
4 shallots, diced
a drizzle of olive oil
12 sole fillets, skinned and trimmed
1kg spinach, trimmed and washed
100ml double cream
sea salt
freshly ground black pepper
lemon juice to finish

Heat a small piece of the butter in a pan, add the shallots and cook gently for 10 minutes over a low heat. Do not allow them to colour.

Meanwhile, set the grill to high. Lightly oil a baking tray and put it under the grill to heat. When the tray is hot, twist the sole fillets and place them in a layer on the tray – you should hear them sizzle as they touch it. Put under the hot grill for 4–5 minutes, then remove them and set the grill to low.

Place the spinach in a large saucepan with 3 tablespoons of water and cook for up to 3 minutes, stirring frequently. The spinach should soften and warm but retain its shape and texture. Put the spinach in a lightly buttered dish and arrange the sole fillets on top. Place under the low grill to keep warm.

Add the cream and seasoning to the shallots and continue to simmer. Cut the remaining butter into small knobs, adding a few pieces at a time to the simmering cream and mixing well with a balloon whisk. When all the butter is added you should have a glossy sauce. Pour the sauce over the spinach and sole and finish with a squeeze of lemon.

Dover sole is superior to lemon sole. It has a firm but delicate texture and an exquisite taste, but with these qualities goes an expensive price tag. Lemon sole is more affordable, but you lose a little refinement in taste and texture.

Grilled Sole with Hollandaise

Sole is a delicious, tender fish which needs very little to enhance it. (See page 93 for a note about sole.) *Sole à l'Hollandaise* is perfect – indeed hollandaise sauce is a perfect accompaniment to all kinds of fish, as well as making asparagus or green beans into an elegant vegetarian starter.

Preparation: 25 minutes
Cooking: 25 minutes

Serves 6

For the hollandaise:
350g butter
2 tbsp white wine vinegar
juice of 1 lemon
6 egg yolks

For the fish:
12 sole fillets
olive oil
sea salt
freshly ground black pepper
a bunch of flat-leaf parsley
3 lemons, halved

First make the sauce. Melt the butter slowly in a saucepan. In a separate, small saucepan, heat the white wine vinegar and lemon juice until just boiling. Place the egg yolks in a jug and blend with a hand-held blender, then slowly add the hot vinegar and lemon juice. Then, just as the butter comes to the boil, slowly pour it into the egg yolks and vinegar, constantly blending until all the butter is incorporated. Place the jug in a basin of hot water and cover until ready to serve. If it is too thick, blend in a dash of water.

Set the grill to hot. Lay the sole fillets on the grill pan, drizzle with olive oil, season and place under the hot grill for 5 minutes. Serve the sole with sprigs of parsley, halves of lemon and the hollandaise sauce.

Simone's Marinated Tuna

Try this great dish, which should be made using only really fresh tuna, with steamed sliced new potatoes and a green salad. One of my great-aunt Simone's favourites, this dish is absurdly simple and quick to make.

Preparation: 10 minutes, plus 12 hours' marinating
Cooking: 8 minutes

Serves 6

6 shallots, finely sliced
zest and juice of 6 lemons
150ml olive oil
2 chillies, red or green, halved, deseeded and diced
sea salt
freshly ground black pepper
6 x 125g tuna fillet, thinly sliced

In a large, low-sided dish mix together the shallots, lemon zest and juice, olive oil, chilli and seasoning. Finally, add the tuna fillets and leave to marinate for 12 hours, turning occasionally.

Heat a grill or barbecue to hot and take the tuna from the marinade. Cook the fish for 1–2 minutes on each side for rare (4 minutes for well done) and serve at once, drizzled with the remaining marinade.

Mullet with a Mustard Crust

Nothing could be easier than this recipe, *Rouget à la Moutarde*, but it is important that the fish is fresh from the sea to retain that perfect flavour. Serve with steamed potatoes and watercress.

Preparation: 10 minutes
Cooking: 20 minutes

Serves 6

6 red mullet, gutted and scaled
2 tbsp Dijon mustard
200g jar grainy mustard (such as Meaux)
olive oil

Heat the oven to 200°C/gas 6.

Make 3 incisions across the fish on each side. Mix the Dijon and grainy mustard and spread thickly all over the fish, pushing some into each of the cuts. Lightly oil a large baking tray, place the fish on it and bake in the top of the oven for 20 minutes. Serve at once.

When I was a child, red mullet were so common on Noirmoutier that you could almost catch them with your hands. It was our staple diet, grilled, barbecued or as the principal ingredient for fish soup. Now these delicious fish are less easy to find, and are becoming quite a delicacy in expensive restaurants.

Poultry

Poultry has always been an important part of the French kitchen, which is hardly surprising in a country with such a strong farming and rural tradition. At one time, every country family kept hens, ducks or geese, and these birds still tend to be associated with peasant dishes. Wild birds, too, have their place, especially in the more southern, mountainous regions of France, but many of these birds are difficult to find in England, and we have adapted some dishes accordingly. Choose your poultry well. It is worth finding a good organic butcher or farmer who can advise and supply you.

The age of the chicken usually determines the method of cooking. Poussin (3 months or less, average weight 400g, serves 2): these birds should be split lengthways and grilled for 10 minutes on each side, or oven-roasted for 20 minutes. The flesh is extremely tender, but has a very light taste. Spring chicken (3–6 months, average weight 800g, serves 4): roast in the oven for 20 minutes per 500g. The flesh is tasty and tender. Pullet (7–8 months, average weight

2–3kg, serves 6): oven- or pot-roasted, the flesh is firm and of superior taste. Hen (12 months or more, average weight 1.5-3kg, serves 4): these birds are perfect for pot-roasting or braising. The taste is excellent, but unless cooked for a long time the flesh can be rather tough. Braise or stew for 3-4 hours. Ideal for country dishes such as *pot-au-feu* or *poule au pot*.

Duck flesh is dark and quite strong in taste. A duckling (2–3 months, average weight 800g) can be pan-fried (10–12 minutes per 500g) or roasted (15 minutes per 500g). An older bird (4 months or more) is better roasted (18 minutes per 500g) or braised (about 3 hours).

Goose is exceptional, but quite rich in fat. Don't be afraid of this; goose fat is wonderful for roasting potatoes and other vegetables. Roast the goose (age 6–8 months minimum, average weight 4–5 kg) for 30 minutes per 500g.

It's best to use young pigeons (3–5 months, average weight, 300g). The flesh is delicate and very slightly gamey, and can be roasted or sautéed (about 30 minutes, one bird serves 2).

These recipes are not designed with
mass-produced poultry in mind. A fresh,
well-fed, free-range chicken is a world away
from a plastic-wrapped, watery chicken fillet.
Similarly, different birds have very different
characteristics, determined by age, species
and diet, and you should bear this in mind when
making your choice.

Madame Douazan's Poule au Pot

This centuries-old dish remains one of the simplest and most traditional methods of cooking chicken. Its patron is King Henri IV, who, concerned at the general poverty of his people, declared that under his reign even the poorest family should be able to have *poule au pot* every Sunday. Many people still use this sixteenth-century recipe, and this is Madame Douazan's version, which I first tried at her home, and which I always associate with her.

The people of Nérac in Gascony, where she lives, have a special affection for Henri IV. He had a castle there, with a wild park, La Garenne, where he spent many summers before coming to the throne. Local folklore has it that one year he fell in love with a girl, Fleurette, who drowned herself when the young Henri deserted her. La Garenne has a fountain with a marble statue in memory of her, and the Nérac chocolaterie, La Cigale, makes the most wonderful little bittersweet chocolates called Amours de Fleurette. They're a romantic lot in Nérac …

Preparation: 35 minutes
Cooking: time: 2 hours

Serves 6

1 x 2–2.5kg free-range chicken
900ml water
300ml white wine
8 shallots, peeled
2 bay leaves
3 sprigs of thyme
6 cloves
sea salt
freshly ground black pepper
12 small potatoes
4 carrots, cut into 5cm lengths, or 12 baby carrots
1 turnip, cut into wedges, or 6 baby turnips
3 leeks, cut into 5cm lengths, or 6 baby leeks
4 sticks of celery, cut into 5cm lengths
1 small cabbage, cored and cut into wedges

For the stuffing:
200g lean pork meat, minced
100g thick-cut bacon, diced
100g chicken livers, roughly chopped
1 egg
2 cloves of garlic, crushed, peeled and chopped
4 shallots, diced
a bunch of flat-leaf parsley, chopped
50g breadcrumbs, made from a dried loaf
sea salt
freshly ground black pepper

First prepare the stuffing. Put the pork, bacon and chicken livers in a bowl. Add the egg, garlic, shallots, parsley, breadcrumbs and seasoning and mix everything together. You get a really good, even mix if you do this with your hands.

Heat the oven to 180°C/gas 4.

Trim the chicken cavity of any excess fat and fill with the stuffing. Close up the neck and tail end of the chicken with a poultry needle and thread or by weaving cocktail sticks through. Place the chicken in a large casserole dish and add the water and wine, shallots, bay leaves, thyme, cloves and seasoning. Cover with a lid and cook in the preheated oven for 1½ hours.

When the hour and a half has elapsed, add the potatoes, carrots and turnip to the chicken in the pot, immerse them in the cooking juices and cook the casserole for a further 15 minutes. Then remove the pot from the oven.

Carefully lift out the chicken and rest it on a wire rack to drain off excess cooking juices. Return these juices to the pot, place the pot over a moderate heat on the hob, add the leeks, celery and cabbage, cover with a lid and simmer for 10 minutes.

While the vegetables are simmering, remove and discard the skin from the chicken, and carve the meat and stuffing.

Scoop the vegetables out of the cooking stock and serve them in individual, deep bowls with the chicken and the stuffing, and a generous ladle of the cooking stock.

Poule au pot is a peasants' dish. It works best with
an older bird, the lengthy cooking bringing out the
stronger flavours. Cooked in this way, the meat
becomes sweet and tender, but it is important to use
a free-range chicken and good quality vegetables.
For maximum authenticity, serve the leftover cooking
stock as a soup starter, with vermicelli.

Garlic Roast Chicken

Garlic and rosemary give this dish, *Poulet à l'Ail*, a lovely Provençal flavour, filling your kitchen with the aromas of summer holidays all year round.

Preparation: 40 minutes
Cooking: 1½–2 hours

Serves 6

3 whole garlic bulbs
1 chicken
4 sprigs of rosemary
1 lemon, sliced
sea salt and freshly ground black pepper
olive oil for drizzling
2 tbsp flour
200ml white wine
a bunch of flat-leaf parsley, finely chopped

Break the garlic cloves away from the bulbs, place in a small saucepan, cover with water and simmer gently with a lid on for 30 minutes. Leave to cool in the water. Drain the garlic cloves but don't throw the water away.

Heat the oven to 180°C/gas 4. Carefully ease the skin of the chicken away from the breasts. Place a sprig of rosemary and a layer of lemon slices between the skin and the meat on each side. Stuff the remaining rosemary and lemon, along with the garlic cloves, into the chicken. Season.

Drizzle a heavy-based roasting tin with olive oil, place the chicken on it and cook it according to weight: 20 minutes per 500g and 20 minutes extra. Transfer the cooked chicken to a serving board and keep it warm while you make the sauce. Place the roasting tin directly over a low heat, add the flour and blend it in well. Slowly pour in the reserved garlic water, stirring constantly. Add most of the white wine, bring to the boil and adjust the consistency with extra wine if desired. Pass through a sieve into a saucepan, add the parsley and bring to a simmer.

Carve the chicken and serve with the sauce.

Country Chicken

This is a simple and tasty way of cooking young chickens, and works very well with rice or pasta.

Preparation: 20 minutes, plus overnight marinating
Cooking: 50 minutes

Serves 6

2 small chickens, cut into 6 pieces each (ask your butcher to do it)
12 shallots, peeled
5 bay leaves
400g thick-cut smoked bacon, chopped
2 tbsp olive oil
sea salt
freshly ground black pepper
2 tbsp grainy mustard (such as Meaux)
a bunch of French tarragon
200ml white wine

Trim the chicken pieces of fat and place them in a bowl. Add the whole shallots, bay leaves, bacon, olive oil and seasoning. Mix well, cover and leave to marinate in the fridge overnight.

Heat the oven to 180°C/gas 4.

Transfer the marinating chicken to a large roasting tin, and spoon its marinade over it. Cook for 40 minutes.

Place the mustard in a bowl. Strip the tarragon leaves from their stalks and chop finely, add to the mustard along with the white wine, and mix well.

Remove the chicken from the oven and drain off the excess fat, then pour the mustard mix over the chicken. Mix well and return to the oven to cook for another 10 minutes.

Coq au Vin: part of a dwindling tradition of old French dishes relying on wine, herbs and a generous cooking time to ensure maximum tenderness and flavour.

Coq au Vin

This is another very old dish, invented – or so the story goes – by Julius Caesar. A group of Gauls had been cornered Asterix-fashion by one of Caesar's garrisons. To prove that they had plenty to eat, the Gauls sent out an old cockerel to the enemy, with a message around its neck saying '*Bon appétit!*' Caesar promptly invited the leaders of the Gaulish tribes to a dinner, in the course of which he served the cockerel (cooked to perfection in wine and rare herbs), promising the Gauls that if they surrendered, he would not only give them the recipe, but personally ensure that they and their descendants ate well and lived in prosperity for ever. Did they believe him? The story doesn't tell … Make this dish the night before serving to let the flavours infuse and intensify.

Preparation: 40 minutes, plus overnight marinating if desired
Cooking: 50 minutes

Serves 6

1 chicken, weighing about 1kg, jointed into 12 pieces (ask your butcher to do this)
500ml red wine
1 tbsp olive oil
150g thick-cut bacon, cubed
12 small shallots, peeled
200g button mushrooms
1 clove of garlic, crushed, peeled and chopped
3 tbsp flour
300ml chicken stock
2 bay leaves
2 sprigs of thyme
sea salt
freshly ground black pepper
a bunch of flat-leaf parsley, chopped

Trim the chicken pieces of excess fat. For a really rich flavour, marinate the chicken pieces in the wine overnight. The next day, pour off the marinade (keep it to cook with) and dry the chicken well with kitchen paper to make frying easier.

Heat the oven to 180°C/gas 4.

Put the olive oil and bacon in a large ovenproof casserole dish and cook over a medium heat for 3 minutes. Add the whole shallots and cook for a further 6 minutes until browned, then add the mushrooms and garlic and cook for another 2 minutes, stirring well. Remove the ingredients from the pan and set to one side.

Place the chicken in the casserole and cook until golden and sealed all over – do this in batches to get a good even colour. Set the browned chicken to one side.

Reduce the heat, add the flour to the pan and allow it to absorb the fat. Don't forget to mix in all the coloured cooking bits on the side of the pan. Slowly stir in the red wine (or reserved marinade) and chicken stock and bring to the boil. Return the chicken, vegetables and bacon to the casserole dish, along with the bay leaves, thyme and seasoning. Cover and cook in the oven for 35 minutes. Just before serving, add the chopped parsley.

Duck Confit Tart

Serve this tart warm, with a green salad alongside.

Preparation: 40 minutes
Cooking: 45 minutes

Serves 6

For the pastry:
250g self-raising flour
125g butter, cut into small pieces
cold water

For the filling:
1 x 400g tin duck or goose *confit*
500g small whole potatoes, cooked
4 eggs
75ml milk
2 tbsp double cream
butter for greasing
4 shallots, diced
2 cloves of garlic, crushed, peeled and chopped
a bunch of flat-leaf parsley, chopped
sea salt
freshly ground black pepper

To make the pastry, put the flour in a bowl, add the butter, and rub together with your fingertips until the mixture resembles breadcrumbs. Using a round-bladed knife in a cutting motion, combine a couple of tablespoons of cold water with the mix until a pastry ball forms. Turn out on a lightly floured surface and quickly knead until the pastry is even and smooth, then wrap and place in the fridge to chill for 30 minutes.

To make the filling, open the tin of *confit* and remove the meat (save the fat, in the fridge, for roasting potatoes). Discard the skin and then roughly chop the meat. Slice the potatoes. In a bowl, beat the eggs with the milk and cream.

Heat the oven to 220°C/gas 7.

Lightly butter a 20–25cm pie dish. Roll out the pastry and use it to line the dish.

Add the confit, shallots, garlic, parsley and seasoning to the pie base, then layer the potatoes over the top. Finally, pour the egg mix over. Cook the pie in the middle of the oven for 45 minutes. Reduce the oven temperature after 30 minutes if the tart is browning too much on top.

Façon Bistrot

des entrées

Pêle mêle de tomates mozzarella au bas
Aiguillette de saumon fumé sur lit de betteraves
Terrine de foies de volaille, compotée d'oignons
                                                    myrtil
...tail de melon et JA MBON d'AOSTE au

This is one of those magical out-of-the-storecupboard dishes – that is, so long as you buy tins of *confit* when you are in France. The dish is straightforward to make and delicious to eat, and you can hunt down tins of *confit* in this country too.

Crunchy Roast Duck with Turnips

The meat content of a whole duck is low, which is why breasts (*magrets*) are so popular, while legs are an economical way to produce a delicious meal. Many different varieties of duck are cooked in France. The renowned breeds are Barbary, which are raised in the wild and have a gentle musky flavour, Nantes (or Challens, named after the marshland area where the duck lives), which has a delicately flavoured flesh, and Rouen, the most well-known, which has an exceptionally fine flesh and a special flavour because it is killed in such a way (smothering) that the blood remains in the muscles.

Preparation: 20 minutes
Cooking: 1 hour 15 minutes

Serves 6

1 tbsp olive oil
6 duck legs
sea salt
freshly ground black pepper
6 shallots, peeled
12 baby turnips, trimmed
1 large cooking apple, peeled, cored and chopped
20g flour
300ml cider
100ml vegetable stock

Heat the oven to 200°C/gas 6.
 Place the olive oil in a large, heavy-based roasting tin and heat in the oven for 5 minutes. Stab the duck legs all over with a fork, rub with seasoning, then place in the roasting tin and cook for 20 minutes. Turn the duck legs, and add the whole shallots and turnips to the roasting tin. Baste with the fat, reduce the heat to 180°C/gas 4 and roast for a further 20 minutes.

Turn the duck legs again, and add the apple, moving the roasting vegetables to ensure they cook evenly. Roast for a further 20 minutes or until the duck is golden and crunchy and the vegetables soft and browned.
 Remove the duck and vegetables from the roasting tin and place them on a warm serving dish. Drain off excess fat (reserve it for roasting or sautéing potatoes) and add the flour to the tin, mixing it in vigorously to make a roux. Then slowly add the cider and vegetable stock, stirring well to mix in the roasting flavours in the pan. Place directly over a medium heat and bring to a simmer, constantly stirring. Check the seasoning, pour over the duck and the roasted vegetables, and serve.

Duck Breasts in Orange

Magrets de Canard à l'Orange is a variation on the classic dish of duck with orange. Duck works well with sweet tastes, and this is a quick and stress-free version to prepare.

Preparation: 20 minutes
Cooking: 25 minutes

Serves 6

6 duck breasts with skin
20g butter
3 oranges
100ml fresh orange juice
1 tbsp vinegar
1 tbsp unrefined caster sugar
1 tbsp cornflour
2 tbsp Grand Marnier

Score the skin of each duck breast in a criss-cross pattern. Melt the butter in a large frying pan and cook the duck breasts, skin-side down, over a medium heat for 10 minutes, until the skin is golden and the fat has run out of it.

Meanwhile, use a sharp knife to peel the oranges down to the flesh, cutting away all the pith (do this over a plate to catch any escaping juice), and then cut into segments between the fine skin. Remove any pips.

Pour the fat away from the pan the duck breasts are cooking in, then cook the breasts, flesh-side down this time but still over a medium heat, for a further 8 minutes. Remove the meat from the pan and slice it, arrange it on a warm plate, top with the orange segments and keep it warm.

Add the orange juice to the pan (including any juice from the plate), along with the vinegar and sugar, and bring to a simmer. Remove from the heat. Mix the cornflour with a little water, add it to the pan and stir well until smooth. Finally pour in the Grand Marnier.

Pour the sauce over the sliced duck breasts and serve.

Fresh Foie Gras with Roasted Peaches

Foie gras has raised temperatures one way or another since Roman times. Horace's early writings describe a method of preparing geese that have been force-fed on figs. In the eleventh century Sainte Radegonde – one of France's many culinary saints – had a dish of *foie gras* prepared for the soon-to be-canonized Bishop of Poitiers, who thanked her with poems and odes in her honour. The marquis of Contades received a large fiefdom in Picardy from Louis XV as thanks for a gift of foie gras prepared by his pastry chef. Today it has become at the same time one of the most sought-after and one of the most vilified foodstuffs in the world, appreciated by gourmets for its incomparable texture and taste, and denounced for the method of its production. It is, however, one of the oldest and most fabled ingredients of the French kitchen, and I'd hate to see political correctness send it into culinary extinction, the way of peacock hearts and larks' tongues in aspic …

Preparation: 10 minutes, plus overnight marinating
Cooking: 25 minutes

Serves 6

1 fresh goose *foie gras* of about 800g
sea salt
freshly ground black pepper
50ml Madeira
50ml cognac
260g butter
5 fresh peaches, each destoned and cut into
8 wedges
a grating of nutmeg

Clean and trim the *foie gras* of any fibres or veins using a thin, sharp-bladed knife. Put it in a dish, add seasoning, Madeira and cognac, cover and marinate in the fridge overnight, turning it when you can in the evening before and the morning after.

The next day, remove the *foie gras* from the marinade and dry well with kitchen paper. Keep the marinade. Slice the *foie gras* into escalopes, each of about 100g.

Heat 100g of the butter in a large frying pan and, over high heat, sear the *foie gras* on each side for 45 seconds – or more if you must. Remove from the pan and keep warm. Add more butter if required and cook the peaches for 2 minutes, still over a high heat. Arrange the peaches on warmed plates and set aside.

Pour the marinade juices into the frying pan, bring to a simmer, then reduce the heat. Cut the remaining butter into small pieces and add it to the pan, whisking vigorously with a balloon whisk, until a glossy sauce is made. Add the nutmeg.

Arrange the *foie gras* on top of the peaches, spoon over the sauce and serve at once.

I picked up this way of cooking fresh *foie gras – Foie Gras Poëlé aux Pêches –* in the Gers, at the home of Madame Consularo, who runs the Château Bellevue in Cazaubon, near Eauze, and does all the cooking herself. She prepared this dish specially for me, and I've never had better.

To flambé is simply to pour spirit over food and ignite it. The flaming dish creates a sensation, but, more than just a show, flambéing wonderfully enhances flavour too. The easiest way is to heat the spirit in a small saucepan, carefully ignite it and then pour the flaming liquid over the dish.

Quails with Cherries

Cailles Flambées is a simple but spectacular dish for a festive meal.

Preparation: 35 minutes
Cooking: 40 minutes

Serves 6

750g sour cherries, pitted
150ml red wine
a pinch of cinnamon
6 quails (your butcher will prepare them for you)
sea salt
freshly ground black pepper
25g butter
1 tbsp cornflour
50ml kirsch
50ml cognac

Take a generous third of the cherries, about 300g, and press them through a sieve to extract the juice. Or whiz the cherries in a blender and then pass them through a fine sieve – this is far quicker. Then put the juice, the remaining whole cherries, the red wine and cinnamon in a small saucepan, bring to the boil and simmer gently for 30 minutes.

Meanwhile, take the quails and season them on the inside. Melt the butter in a large pan, add the quails and cook them for 20 minutes until browned all over.

Add the cherry mix and juice to the quails, cover them and simmer for another 15 minutes, turning the quails halfway through cooking.

Remove the quails from the sauce and place on a warmed serving dish. Use a slotted spoon to remove the cherries, and scatter them over the quails. Set aside a spoonful of the liquid to cool. Then increase the heat under the remaining sauce to reduce it. Mix the cornflour with the cooled liquid, remove the sauce from the heat and quickly stir in the cornflour until smooth and blended. Return the sauce to the heat, stirring constantly until it thickens.

Pour the sauce over the quails, then heat and ignite the kirsch and cognac to flambé the dish just before serving (see the facing page).

Pigeon meat is tender and only slightly gamey, and the peas give it a succulent sweetness. Use young pigeons for this delicious dish, or try poussins for another version of it.

Pigeon with Peas

Ideally, you should use 4–5 month old pigeons and freshly shelled, small peas for this traditional recipe, *Pigeon aux Petits Pois*. For the bouquet garni, tie together a bundle of fresh herbs. I use sprigs of parsley, thyme, sage and rosemary, 2 bay leaves and a 5cm piece of leek.

Preparation: 15 minutes
Cooking: 30 minutes

Serves 6

70g butter
100g thick-cut bacon, cut into strips
8 shallots, finely diced
3 pigeons, cut in half (ask the butcher to do this)
100ml white wine
1 litre chicken stock
1 bouquet garni
sea salt
freshly ground black pepper
1kg freshly shelled peas
10g unrefined brown sugar
1 soft lettuce, such as Batavia or butterhead (Webbs), finely sliced
5 spring onions, finely sliced
a bunch of mint, finely chopped

Melt the butter in a large saucepan, add the bacon and shallots and cook until just golden, then remove from the pan with a slotted spoon. Add the pigeons and lightly brown all over on the outside. Add the white wine, stock, bouquet garni and seasoning, then return the cooked bacon and shallots and bring to the boil. Simmer for 15 minutes.

Add the peas, sugar and lettuce, stir well and simmer for a further 15 minutes, turning the pigeons so that they cook evenly.

Add the spring onions for the final 2 minutes of cooking. Serve garnished with freshly chopped mint leaves.

Christmas Turkey with Chestnuts

The traditional French Christmas meal takes place on Christmas Eve, and lasts long into the night. It's more usual to make this dish with goose, but you can use turkey – *Dinde aux Marrons* – as long as you ensure the meat doesn't dry out. For me, chestnuts have always evoked the spirit of the season, and in France they are often used as a main vegetable rather than simply a garnish. They have a sweetness that works very well with roasted meat, and, fortunately, using the tinned ones is just as good as buying them fresh. As for the turkey, to get one with its giblets you need to go to a good butcher who buys from small producers. Whether you can get a turkey with its giblets will tell you a great deal about the quality of your butcher.

Preparation: 20 minutes
Turkey cooking time: 20 minutes per 500g

Serves 8 to 10

For the stuffing:
2 x 450g packets or tins peeled chestnuts
500g sausagemeat
4 shallots, finely diced
2 cloves of garlic, crushed, peeled and chopped
a bunch of flat-leaf parsley, chopped
a bunch of sage, chopped
sea salt
freshly ground black pepper
1 egg

For the turkey:
1 x 4kg turkey with its giblets (if possible)
100g butter
6 sticks of celery, halved
6 carrots, peeled
6 red onions, peeled
100ml white wine
1 litre chicken or turkey stock
25g flour

Heat the oven to 180°C/gas 4.

To make the stuffing, slice half the chestnuts finely and place them in a bowl with the sausagemeat, shallots, garlic, parsley, sage, seasoning and egg. Mix well – this is best done using your hands.

Remove the giblets from the turkey and place to one side, then season the inside of the turkey and stuff with the freshly made mixture. Generously smear the outside of the turkey with butter.

Grease a heavy-based, deep roasting tin with a little of the remaining butter and add the giblets, celery and the whole carrots and onions. Pour over half the wine and half the chicken stock, and place the turkey on top. Cover generously with tin foil and cook in the middle of the oven for 1½ hours.

Remove the turkey from the oven and reduce the heat to 150°C/gas 2. Add the whole chestnuts and the remaining wine and stock, smear the turkey again with what remains of the butter, re-cover and return to the oven for a further 1–1½ hours. For the final 10 minutes of cooking, remove the tin foil and increase the heat to 180°C/gas 4 to give the turkey a golden skin. Remove from the oven, lift the turkey onto a carving plate and leave to rest in a warm place for 10–15 minutes – this allows the meat to relax and become more tender.

Discard the giblets. Carefully lift out the vegetables and chestnuts from the roasting tin and keep warm. Place the roasting tin directly on the heat and, using a flour dredger, shake in about 1 tablespoon of flour. Whisk vigorously and bring to the boil to make a coating gravy – adjust with more liquid (stock or water) or a little more flour to get the right consistency. Pass through a fine sieve, then check the seasoning. Serve the turkey with the chestnuts and vegetables and sauce.

Meat

Most French families now rely on simple grilled or roasted meats, with little accompaniment other than a sauce made from the meat's own juices. However, many traditional dishes rely on sauces and long cooking times for their success. The following dishes are old favourites which have been slightly adapted to make them easier to make, but which still convey some of the many textures, smells and tastes of the traditional French kitchen.

The essential thing when buying meat is to ensure it is of excellent quality. I find that, as with poultry, free-range organic meat is greatly superior in taste to the pre-packed, mass-produced variety. Befriend a good organic butcher, who will be able to recommend cuts of meat to suit the recipe you are planning, and bear in mind that whatever your personal standpoint on eating meat (and be it on ethical, taste or health grounds), it is always beneficial to know that what you are eating has been treated with respect before it reaches your table.

The French have a good tradition of local butchers who will advise and, if necessary, prepare your meat for you. Our local butcher used to come in a van and deliver the Sunday roast to us at my grandfather's house.

Paupiettes au Vin Blanc is one of my mother's recipes, which I associate with leisurely Sunday lunches in France with my grandparents. You can buy *paupiettes* ready-made in France, but they are quite easy to make at home – as our recipe demonstrates – and well worth the effort.

Veal Parcels in White Wine Sauce

The secret of this dish is in the cooking time: the longer you cook it, the better it gets, and if you make it the night before, the flavours will marry and intensify overnight, making a richer and tastier sauce.

Preparation: 40 minutes
Cooking: 1 hour 15 minutes

Serves 6

For the filling:
2 tbsp olive oil
100g mushrooms, chopped
1 red onion, diced
60g minced pork
2 cloves of garlic, crushed, peeled and chopped
a small bunch of flat-leaf parsley, chopped
a small bunch of sage, chopped
sea salt
freshly ground black pepper
30g breadcrumbs

For the veal:
6 thin veal escalopes
25g butter
3 red onions, peeled and cut in half
25g flour
500ml white wine
6 small carrots, peeled
600g new potatoes, peeled

Heat the oven to 180°C/gas 4.

Make the filling for the veal parcels: heat the olive oil in a frying pan, and sauté the mushrooms and the diced onion for 5 minutes. Add the pork, garlic, parsley, sage and seasoning, mix well and cook for another 5 minutes. Then remove from the heat, mix in the breadcrumbs and leave to cool a little.

Lay out the veal escalopes on the work surface and divide the filling among them. Fold in the ends and then roll up each escalope, tying with string to make little parcels.

Heat the butter in a frying pan and fry the veal parcels together with the halved red onions until the veal is golden. Remove the onions and veal and place in a casserole dish.

Add the flour to the pan where the escalopes were fried and stir it in well, gathering all the tasty bits into the mix. Then slowly add the white wine, stirring well, and bring to the boil. Take the sauce off the heat, pass it through a sieve, and pour it over the veal and onions.

Put the casserole in the oven and cook for 20 minutes. Take the casserole out, put in the carrots and potatoes, cover with a lid, and cook for a further 55 minutes. Serve hot.

Lentil and Toulouse Sausage Casserole

This casserole, *Lentilles-Saucisses à l'Ancienne*, is another old favourite: easy to make, completely stress-free and very versatile. It's great with country bread and strong red wine if you want a hot meal in a hurry. Toulouse sausages are made with pure pork and a generous amount of garlic. They vary from shop to shop according to personal recipes, so keep trying until you find your perfect one, or, if you prefer, use any other favourite sausage.

Preparation: 20 minutes, plus overnight soaking
Cooking: 40 minutes

Serves 6

300g green or brown lentils
2 tbsp olive oil
2 onions, diced
3 sticks of celery, chopped
2 cloves of garlic, crushed, peeled and chopped
3 sprigs of thyme
1 bay leaf
3 large tomatoes, peeled and chopped
2 tsp tomato purée
200ml red wine
400ml water, approximately
6 Toulouse or other favourite sausages, weighing about 750g in total
a large bunch of flat-leaf parsley

Soak the lentils overnight in water, then drain them and set them aside.

Heat the oven to 200°C/gas 6.

Heat the olive oil in a casserole dish, add the onion, celery and garlic and sauté for 5 minutes. Add the thyme leaves (stripped from the stalks), bay leaf, tomatoes and purée, mix together and cook for 5 minutes. Remove from the heat, add the lentils and red wine, stir well, then pour in enough water to cover. Place the sausages on top, cover with a lid and cook in the oven for 30 minutes. Stir in the parsley just before serving.

LE
ST. VINCENT

SANDWICHERIE

Smoked Ham Winter Pot

Potée Auvergnate is a traditional French country dish. Every region has its variants, depending on the available vegetables, but this one is southern in character, thickened with chunky haricot beans and potatoes, perfect with a bottle of characterful red wine and an open fire …

Preparation: 40 minutes, plus overnight soaking
Cooking: 2 hours 15 minutes

Serves 6

500g haricot beans
1.5kg piece of smoked ham
6 small red onions, peeled
2 cloves of garlic, crushed, peeled and chopped
1 bay leaf
a sprig of thyme
freshly ground black pepper
1 tbsp Dijon mustard
6 carrots, cut into 5cm pieces
500g small to medium waxy potatoes, peeled but left whole
3 leeks, cut into 5cm pieces
sea salt
200g green beans, topped and tailed
a large bunch of flat-leaf parsley, finely chopped

Soak the haricot beans overnight in water. The next day drain and rinse them well.

Place the ham in a large casserole pot, cover with water and bring to a simmer, then cook for 10 minutes before draining and discarding the water. Return the ham to the casserole along with the onions, garlic, haricot beans, bay leaf, thyme, pepper and Dijon mustard. Just cover with water, gently bring up to the boil, skim off any residue and simmer for 1½ hours with the lid on.

After the hour and a half has elapsed, add the carrots, potatoes and leeks to the casserole, cover and simmer for another 15 minutes.

Check the seasoning – you may not need to add salt. Add the green beans and parsley and cook for a further 5 minutes.

Lift out the ham, allow all the stock to run back into the casserole, and place the ham on a large carving board or plate. Slice the ham and serve it with the vegetables and cooking stock.

Pork with Blackcurrant

Porc au Cassis is easy to make, and the result is a wonderfully intense concentration of autumn flavours.

Preparation: 25 minutes
Cooking: 30 minutes

Serves 6

400g blackcurrants (frozen if out of season)
2 tbsp unrefined sugar
50ml water
1 tbsp olive oil
2 pork fillets, about 875g together, trimmed of fat
sea salt
freshly ground black pepper
60g butter
2 large cooking apples, peeled, cored and sliced
a pinch of cinnamon
1 tsp blackcurrant jam

Wash fresh blackcurrants, remove any stems, and place the fruit (fresh or frozen) in a small saucepan with the sugar and water. Cover and gently bring to boiling point, then remove from the heat. When they have cooled a little, drain the blackcurrants, reserving the juice. Set the juice and the blackcurrants aside.

Heat the oil in a sauté pan and fry the pork fillets over a medium heat until golden all over. Season, then cover and cook for another 15 minutes. When cooked, remove them from the pan and allow them to rest.

Meanwhile, heat 10g of the butter in a saucepan and fry the apples gently for 10 minutes or until golden. Add the cinnamon.

Put the reserved blackcurrant juice and the jam in the pan the pork was cooked in, bring to the boil and simmer. Cut the remaining butter into pieces and whisk it in, simmering rapidly, until a glossy sauce is made. Add the blackcurrants.

Slice the pork fillets and serve on a bed of the sautéed apples, topped with the blackcurrant sauce.

The sharpness of the blackcurrants cuts through the richness of the pork in this dish. It works well on its own, as above, or with steamed potatoes, which do not interfere with the balance of the dish.

Pork with Lentils

This simple dish, *Porc aux Lentilles*, combines Puy lentils and mustard to make a rich, creamy sauce. Puy lentils are grown only in the Velay region of France, and are famous for their green marbled appearance and excellent flavour. Here they carry the delicious sauce that goes so well with pork.

Preparation: 30 minutes
Cooking: 35 minutes

Serves 6

2 pork fillets, about 875g together, trimmed of fat
a bunch of sage
2 cloves of garlic, peeled and cut into slivers
1 lemon, from which small pieces of rind are cut
sea salt
freshly ground black pepper
1 tbsp olive oil
8 slices smoked streaky bacon, rind removed
1 litre chicken stock
250g Puy lentils
100ml white wine
100ml double cream or crème fraiche
1 tbsp Dijon mustard

Heat the oven to 180°C/gas 4.

Make slits in the pork with a small sharp knife and insert sage leaves, garlic slivers and pieces of lemon rind, then rub with seasoning.

Oil a baking tray with olive oil. Wrap the bacon around the pork. Place the bacon-wrapped fillets on the tray and cook for 35 minutes.

Put the chicken stock and lentils in a large saucepan and simmer gently for 30 minutes until the stock is absorbed. In another pan, combine the white wine, cream, mustard and seasoning and heat through gently. Slice the pork and serve with the lentils and mustard sauce.

Pork Chops with Mustard

Côtelettes de Porc à la Moutarde: a quick and easy way to make simple pork chops special. Good with Sauté Potatoes (page 167). For a real treat, include kidneys with pork chops.

Preparation: 15 minutes
Cooking: 35 minutes

Serves 6

6 pork chops
sea salt
100g butter
3 onions, finely diced
100ml white wine
2 tbsp Dijon mustard
100g small gherkins, sliced

Sprinkle the chops with salt. Melt 30g butter in a large frying pan, add the chops and cook for 12 minutes a side until golden brown all over.

Remove the pork chops from the pan and keep them warm. Add the onions to the pan and sauté over a gentle heat – do not frizzle or brown them. Pour in the white wine, increase the heat and reduce the sauce by half.

Mix in the mustard, reduce the heat again, then add the remaining butter in small pieces. Use a balloon whisk to form a smooth glossy sauce. Finally, stir in the gherkins and serve the sauce with the pork chops.

Roast Pork with Figs

For a perfect crunchy crackling, ask your butcher to score the pork skin in a close criss-cross pattern.

Preparation: 30 minutes
Cooking: 2 hours

Serves 6

2 tbsp olive oil
1¹/₂ kg boned and rolled loin of pork, skin well scored
fine sea salt
freshly ground black pepper
20 ripe figs
200ml white wine
100ml water
20g flour
100ml vegetable water

Heat the oven to 200°C/gas 6.

Put the olive oil in a large, heavy-based roasting tin and heat it in the oven. Rub the scored pork with salt and pepper. Take the tin out of the oven, put in the pork and roll it in the hot oil to cover it evenly. Return the tin to the oven and cook the pork for 40 minutes, then reduce the temperature to 180°C/gas 4 and cook it for a further 40 minutes. At this point, return the oven to its original temperature of 200°C/gas 6: this will help to get that final crunch on the crackling.

Take the tin out of the oven, prick the figs all over with a fork and place them around the roasting pork, add half the white wine and all of the water, and return the tin to the hot oven. After 15 minutes, remove it from the oven and baste the figs with the cooking juices, then return and cook for a further 10 minutes.

Remove from the oven. Transfer the pork to a warm carving board or plate and allow it to rest for 10 minutes in a warm place. Remove the figs and keep them warm.

Make a sauce with the cooking juices from the figs and pork: sprinkle the flour into the roasting tin and stir it well to absorb the oils and juices. Over a low to medium heat, gradually add the remaining white wine and the vegetable water to the paste, mixing well. Allow to simmer and thicken. Check the seasoning, adjust the consistency if necessary with extra water and pass through a sieve.

Carve the pork and serve it with the figs. Serve the sauce separately or poured over the figs.

If you travel to Mont Saint-Michel, you will see the
lambs grazing on the very green marshland by the
water's edge, or even nibbling on the seaweed
growing on the rocks.

Lamb Chops Vert Pré

The crisp, fresh watercress is an excellent accompaniment to tender lamb and new potatoes (Jersey Royals are terrific with this). Traditionally, the lambs are fed on the grass of reclaimed land by the sea, and have a delicate, slightly salty taste, hence the name: *Côtelettes d'Agneau Vert Pré*. A perfect dish for springtime.

Preparation: 15 minutes
Cooking: 30 minutes

Serves 6

500g new potatoes, washed
12 lamb chops
sea salt
freshly ground black pepper
100g butter, softened
a bunch of curly parsley, finely chopped
juice of 1/2 lemon
200g watercress, trimmed

Simmer the new potatoes for 20 minutes or until cooked.

Set the grill to hot. Arrange the chops in the grill pan, sprinkle with seasoning and cook under the hot grill: 6 minutes each side for rare, 8 minutes for medium and 10 minutes for well done.

Cut the butter into knobs, place in a bowl with the finely chopped parsley, lemon juice and seasoning, and mix well.

Arrange the potatoes and watercress on plates, top with the lamb chops and scoops of the butter, and serve.

Lamb Navarin

This dish would originally have been made with mutton, which would have needed a longer cooking time, but this version, *Navarin d'Agneau*, uses lamb for a sweet and tender casserole.

Preparation: 30 minutes
Cooking: 1 hour 40 minutes

Serves 6

2 kg boneless leg or shoulder of lamb, cubed
3 tbsp flour
3 tbsp olive oil
1 litre vegetable stock
2 cloves of garlic, crushed and peeled
6 shallots, peeled and left whole
2 x 410g cans chopped tomatoes or 800g fresh tomatoes, peeled
1 tbsp tomato purée
150ml red wine
2 bay leaves
2 sprigs of marjoram
$1/2$ tsp smoked sweet paprika
sea salt
freshly ground black pepper
200g small carrots
200g small turnips
300g new potatoes

Trim the lamb of any fat. Place in a bowl with the flour and toss to coat the cubes of meat evenly. Heat the olive oil in a large casserole dish, add just enough meat to cover the bottom of the pan and brown the meat all over. Remove and repeat with the next batch, until all the meat is browned. Return all the meat to the pan, add the stock, and bring to a simmer, mixing well. Add the garlic, shallots, chopped tomatoes, purée, red wine, bay leaves, marjoram, paprika and seasoning. Bring to boiling point and simmer gently for 1 hour, stirring from time to time.

Add the whole, prepared carrots, turnips and potatoes to the casserole, making sure they are covered in liquid. You may need to add a little more stock or water at this point. Cook for a further 20 minutes or until the vegetables are soft, then serve.

APÉRITIF
LILLET

S'il vous plaît...

FORMULE LUNCH

Lillet Blanc, Rouge ... Le verre ....

ENTREE ou DESSERT
+
PLAT   19€
+
1 Verre de vin

(au choix dans le Marché

Braised Lamb Shanks

The dish has to be cooked slowly and gently for maximum flavour and tenderness. Serve with mashed potato.

Preparation: 20 minutes, plus marinating overnight
Cooking: 2 hours 10 minutes

Serves 6

For the marinade:
4 cloves of garlic, crushed and peeled
1 tbsp dried juniper berries
zest of 1 lemon
10 shallots, peeled and left whole
1 sprig of rosemary
350ml red wine
sea salt
freshly ground black pepper

For the lamb:
6 lamb shanks
3 tbsp olive oil
10 plum tomatoes, peeled
40g flour
120ml red wine
a bunch of flat-leaf parsley, chopped

Prepare the marinade: put the garlic, juniper berries, lemon zest, shallots, rosemary and red wine in a large, shallow dish. Add seasoning, then put in the lamb shanks and turn them to coat them well. Leave to marinate overnight.

The next day, heat the oven to 180°C/gas 4.

Lightly oil a heavy-based roasting tray. Transfer the lamb shanks and marinade to the tray, cover and cook for 1 hour. Remove from the oven, turn the shanks and add the plum tomatoes. Return to the oven and cook for a further hour, until the meat is soft and tender.

When ready to serve, remove the shanks from the pan and keep them warm while you make the sauce. Put the roasting tray over a low heat, sprinkle in the flour and blend it with all the cooking juices. Gradually whisk in the red wine, bring to the boil, then stir in the parsley. Pour over the lamb shanks and tomatoes and serve.

White Pudding with Truffled Pasta

In France white pudding is often given to children, and it remains one of the great memory dishes of my childhood, simply grilled or fried and eaten with buttered pasta. This rather more grown-up version – *Boudin Blanc aux Tagliatelles Truffées* – uses white truffle, which gives it a sophisticated, earthy flavour.

Preparation: 10 minutes
Cooking: 20 minutes

Serves 6

6 white puddings
600g fresh ribbon pasta
2 tbsp truffle oil
sea salt
freshly ground black pepper
1 white truffle

Heat the grill to medium.

Place the white puddings on the grill pan and cook for 12 minutes or until golden brown, turning occasionally.

Meanwhile, bring a large pan of water to the boil, add the pasta and cook according to packet or shop instructions. Drain and shake the colander to remove every last drop of water.

Warm a large serving dish. Pour half of the truffle oil and a little seasoning into the dish and turn to coat the inside. Add the pasta, drizzle over the remaining oil and sprinkle with a little more seasoning. Toss well.

Slice the white pudding. Finely slice the white truffle using a truffle slicer. Add both to the pasta and serve at once.

Black Pudding and Apple

A classic Breton combination, *Boudin aux Pommes* is terrific with buckwheat pancakes (page 49) or sautéd potatoes, and a crisp green side salad. *Boudin noir*, French black pudding, is very simply made from seasoned pig's blood and fat, with regional additions that can vary from cooked onions to grated raw onions or even apples, prunes or chestnuts.

Preparation: 20 minutes
Cooking: 15 minutes

Serves 6

olive oil for frying
6 black puddings, cut into 2.5cm slices
3 thick rashers bacon, chopped
25g butter
5 Bramley apples, peeled, cored and cut into wedges
pinch of freshly grated nutmeg
sea salt
freshly ground black pepper

Heat a drizzle of oil in a large frying pan, add the black pudding and bacon and cook over a medium-high heat for 2 minutes on each side. Then reduce the heat to low.

While the black pudding and bacon cook, melt the butter in another frying pan, add the apple and nutmeg, mix, and cook on a high heat for about 4 minutes or until the apple colours and just softens.

Add the apple to the black pudding and bacon, season and cook for 5 more minutes over the low heat, then serve.

White pudding – *boudin blanc* – is a little harder to find in Britain than in France (although it's easy to get hold of in Ireland), but it is worth pestering your butcher for. It's white sausage, particularly associated with Christmas, and made from finely ground poultry, veal, pork or rabbit, mixed with spices and cream.

Fillet Steak with Tarragon

This simple but effective way of preparing steaks dates back to the seventeenth century. Use lots of fresh tarragon for a sharp and delicious contrast with the creamy sauce. Try to buy French tarragon: it has a fine, aniseed-like flavour.

Preparation: 10 minutes
Cooking: 10 minutes

Serves 6

25g butter
6 open flat mushrooms
olive oil for frying
4 shallots, diced
100ml white wine
50ml double cream
1 tbsp grainy mustard (such as Meaux)
1 clove of garlic, crushed, peeled and chopped
a bunch of French tarragon, chopped
sea salt
freshly ground black pepper
6 x 150g fillet steaks

Melt the butter in a frying pan over a medium heat and cook the mushrooms on both sides until golden. Reduce the heat and keep warm until needed.

Heat a little olive oil in a saucepan over a medium heat and fry the shallots until soft and golden. Add the wine and simmer for 3 minutes, then reduce the heat and add the cream, mustard, garlic, tarragon and seasoning, and gently warm through. Do not allow to boil.

Heat a drizzle of olive oil in a large frying pan over a high heat and fry the steaks: 1^1/$_2$ minutes each side for rare, 2^1/$_2$ minutes each side for medium and 3 minutes each side for well done (if you must!).

Serve the steaks on the cooked mushrooms topped with the sauce.

This dish must have been a blessing for seventeenth-century chefs. It takes scarcely any time to cook, but is sophisticated enough to please the most exacting nobleman.

Boeuf en Daube

This is the most traditional of the inland Provençal dishes. According to the old story, it was invented by a farmer's wife, who, having put a piece of beef in the oven to cook, began gossiping with a friend, lost track of time, and found the pot dry and the meat burnt. In an attempt to save dinner, she added more water into the pot, but forgot it again and it burnt a second time. Desperate to hide her mistake, the farmer's wife added herbs, wine and vegetables to the pot, so that by the end of the day the resulting dish was so sweet and tender that all her neighbours wanted the recipe. The secret is in the cooking time. My great-grandmother used to cook it in an earthenware pot at a very low heat for three days, but this version has been reduced to a more manageable three and a half hours. Serve with new season boiled potatoes or noodles tossed in a little butter.

Preparation: 30 minutes, plus overnight marinating
Cooking: 3 1/2 hours

Serves 6

For the casserole:
1.75kg piece of rump steak
4 tbsp olive oil
2 onions, sliced
2 cloves of garlic, crushed, peeled and chopped
3 tbsp flour, plus more for dusting
1 tbsp drained capers
100g black olives
1 x 410g tin chopped tomatoes
zest of 1 orange
200g carrots, chopped into 5cm pieces
125g small brown mushrooms
a bunch of flat-leaf parsley

For the marinade:
1 bottle white wine
2 bay leaves
sea salt
freshly ground black pepper

Combine the marinade ingredients in a large bowl, add the rump steak and cover. Leave to marinate overnight, turning from time to time in the evening and during the following day.

Remove the beef from the marinade and pat it dry with kitchen paper. Retain the marinade.

Heat 2 tablespoons of the olive oil in a casserole pan over a low-medium heat. Add the onions and garlic and sauté gently for 8 minutes. Sprinkle in the flour and mix well, then pour in the marinade a little at a time, stirring constantly. When all the liquid has been stirred in, add the capers, olives, tomatoes and orange zest, and allow to simmer.

Heat the oven to 140°C/gas 1.

Heat the remaining olive oil in a frying pan over a high heat. Dust the rump of beef in flour and add it to the hot oil. Brown all over to seal.

Transfer the beef to the casserole and ladle some of the juice back to the frying pan to lift off the delicious meaty bits from the side of the pan. Return the juice to the casserole. Bring the casserole to a simmer, cover with a lid, place in the oven and cook for 2 hours.

When the 2 hours are up, add the carrots and mushrooms and then cook for a further hour.

To serve, lift the beef out on to a carving plate and carve it into thickish slices. Stir the parsley into the vegetables and juices, check the seasoning and spoon it over the slices of beef.

Rabbit with Chestnut Purée

Rabbit has always been a staple in France, and although in England it has been out of favour for many years, it has finally begun to make a comeback. This recipe – *Lapin à la Purée de Marrons* – makes the most of the rich, dark flesh of the rabbit and the sweet flouriness of the chestnuts. This is a perfect dish for autumn.

Preparation: 15 minutes
Cooking: 1 hour

Serves 6

1 rabbit, cut into 6 joints (ask your butcher)
sea salt
freshly ground black pepper
80g butter
150g thick-cut bacon, finely chopped
1 tin puréed chestnuts (unsweetened)
300ml chicken stock
200ml white wine
200g watercress

Heat the oven to 180°C/gas 4.

Take the rabbit joints and season them. Melt the butter in a large casserole, add the rabbit along with the bacon, and toss to coat with the butter. Cover and cook in the oven for 20 minutes, then turn the rabbit, return the lid and cook for a further 20 minutes.

Remove the rabbit and set it aside in a warm place. Add the chestnut purée, stock and wine to the casserole dish, place it over a medium heat and bring it to the boil. Use a balloon whisk to work the purée into the mix, making a rich sauce.

Serve the roasted rabbit with the chestnut sauce on a bed of watercress.

Rabbit with Red Rice

A warming country dish, in which the red rice absorbs and enriches the flavours of wine and rabbit.

Preparation: 20 minutes
Cooking: 1 hour 45 minutes

Serves 6

2 tbsp olive oil
1 rabbit, cut into 6 joints (ask your butcher)
1 red onion, diced
2 sprigs of thyme
1 bay leaf
225g red rice
1 whole garlic bulb, cut in half crossways and roasted (see page 40)
500g plum tomatoes, peeled, quartered and deseeded
100ml white wine
sea salt
freshly ground black pepper

Heat the oven to 150°C/gas 2.

Heat the olive oil in a large casserole over a medium heat. Add the rabbit joints, brown all over – about 10 minutes – then remove. Add the onion, thyme sprigs and bay leaf to the casserole and sauté for 2 minutes. Add the red rice, stirring well to coat the grains in oil and juices, then return the rabbit. Ease the garlic flesh out of its skin and stir it into the casserole with the tomatoes, wine and seasoning. Add water so that the rice is covered with liquid. Mix well, bring to the boil and reduce the heat to very low. Put the lid on and cook for 30 minutes. Stir from time to time and check that the rice does not stick to the bottom of the pan: add a little more wine, or water, if the rice threatens to stick. Serve at once.

Red rice, grown in the Camargue region of France, is nuttier in flavour than ordinary arborio rice, but does not demand as much cooking time as brown rice. It gives a lovely rich colour to this autumn dish.

Vegetables

Traditionally, French dishes were not served with vegetables unless these were an integral part of the dish (such as *Pigeon aux Petits Pois*, *Dinde aux Marrons*). Vegetable dishes would be served as a separate course, although nowadays this is not as common as it once was. As a result, there are many traditional French vegetable-based dishes that can very easily be adapted as main courses for people who prefer not to eat meat or fish.

Living as I do with two strict vegetarians, I find that vegetable dishes play a much greater part in my life than they did in my mother's. It's very hard to be vegetarian in France – although the markets are filled with the most fabulous produce – because to most French people the ethos of vegetarianism is incomprehensible and foreign (my mother still looks at Anouchka with suspicion, and asks her if she is eating properly, although you've never seen such a disgustingly healthy child).

I am quite happy to prepare and eat vegetarian food at home (although many non-vegetarian French dishes have too many personal and cultural associations for me ever to forsake them completely). However, as with all the recipes in this book, the quality of the ingredients is the secret to the success of the dish. Locally grown produce in season is by far the best, and you should try to make the most of it whenever possible. There is little to beat the taste of freshly picked green peas, or buttered new potatoes, or fresh, tender green beans, or sun-warmed tomatoes drizzled with lemon juice and oil.

And as in so many things to do with food, the anticipation – waiting for the strawberries or the young sprouting broccoli to come into season; enjoying the autumn flavours of pumpkin or blackberries or squash – becomes a significant part of the pleasure …

French markets are one of the great pleasures of the summer. Stalls of brightly coloured fruit and vegetables, spices, olives and mushrooms are as much a delight to the eyes as to the palate, and in the warmth of the morning sun, the scent is heavenly.

Anouchka's Pumpkin Seed Mushrooms

My daughter invented this recipe when she was three years old by accidentally dropping the contents of a box of pumpkin seeds into a dish I was preparing. The child shows promise … Serve with jacket potatoes, pasta or on toast with a green salad.

Preparation: 10 minutes
Cooking: 15 minutes

Serves 6

300g brown cap mushrooms
olive oil
25g butter
4 shallots, chopped
3 cloves of garlic, crushed, peeled and chopped
25g pumpkin seeds
sea salt
freshly ground black pepper
juice of 1/2 lemon
150ml white wine
2 tsp grainy mustard (such as Meaux)
3 tbsp double cream

Separate the stems and caps of the mushrooms. Finely chop the stems and slice the tops.

Heat a little oil with the butter in a large frying pan and cook the mushrooms over a medium heat, stirring constantly, until they are golden brown: about 8 minutes. Add the shallots, garlic and pumpkin seeds and cook for a further 4 minutes. Add the seasoning, lemon juice and wine, simmer for 4 minutes, then stir in the mustard and cream. Stir well, allow to simmer for 2 minutes, and then serve.

Imbach Mushrooms

When I was small we sometimes went hunting for mushrooms in the woods with our friends, the Imbachs. I don't remember actually finding any myself (except for once when I found a puffball the size of a beach-ball, and was very disappointed to be told we couldn't eat it), but that didn't stop me trying. This dish is great with any kind of mushrooms, although the larger ones do tend to have more flavour.

Preparation: 10 minutes, plus 1 hour's marinating
Cooking: 8 minutes

Serves 6

12 open, flat mushrooms, or other favourites
6 tbsp olive oil
3 cloves of garlic, crushed, peeled and chopped
200ml red wine
5 tbsp cognac
sea salt
freshly ground black pepper
large bunch of flat-leaf parsley, finely chopped
6 slices of baguette

Place the mushrooms, olive oil, garlic, wine, cognac and seasoning in a large bowl and toss well to coat evenly. Leave to marinate for 1 hour.

Heat the oven to 180°C/gas 4.

Put the mushrooms with their marinade on a roasting tray and cook for 6 minutes, then turn them over and cook for a further 4 minutes. Move the mushrooms around to ensure even cooking.

Sprinkle the parsley over the mushrooms and return to the oven for another 2 minutes.

Lightly toast the slices of baguette. Pile the mushrooms on to the warm bread and drizzle with any cooking juices.

This dish is perfect to make with autumn field mushrooms, and tastes so good that I can quite happily eat it as a main course with a green salad. Cep (porcini) mushrooms – *Boletus edulis* – also work very well prepared in this way, if you are lucky enough to find some, or you could try a mixture of wild and cultivated mushrooms.

Although this is, strictly speaking, an Italian dish, I couldn't resist including it here as it is one of the great comfort foods of winter. I like to make it with the local Noirmoutier potatoes, an ancient variety dating back to the sixteenth century, and perfect for this dish.

Spinach Gnocchi

This is a great cold-weather dish: rich, warm and flavoursome. Ideal for lazy nights in.

Preparation: 40 minutes
Cooking: 30 minutes

Serves 6

600g floury potatoes, peeled and cut into pieces
350g spinach, trimmed and washed
150g flour, plus extra for dusting
1 egg yolk
sea salt
freshly ground black pepper
75g butter
100g blue vein cheese
a bunch of basil

Place the potatoes in a saucepan of boiling water and simmer for 20 minutes. Drain, return to the pan over a low heat and, shaking the pan, allow the excess moisture to steam off. Mash the potatoes until smooth.

Cook the spinach in a large pan over a medium heat with no added moisture, mixing constantly until wilted and soft. When cooked, place in a clean kitchen cloth. Gather the corners together and twist tightly to squeeze out every last drop of moisture, then finely chop the spinach.

Place the mashed potatoes, spinach, flour, egg yolk and seasoning in a large bowl and mix until evenly blended and a soft pliable dough forms. Dust your hands and a board or tray with flour. Take small nuggets of the dough, roll it into balls and place them on the board. You should end up with about 60. Using a fork, gently flatten each ball, allowing the tines of the fork to make indentations across the top.

Heat a large pan of water just to boiling point then reduce the heat. To the simmering water add just enough gnocchi so that they have room to roam around, and cook for 2 minutes or until they rise to the surface. Remove and drain well, and cook the next batch.

Heat the oven to 180°C/gas 4. Lightly butter a large low-sided ovenproof dish.

Place a layer of the cooked gnocchi in the dish, then crumble in some of the blue cheese. Continue to layer the gnocchi and cheese, adding seasoning and the remaining butter cut up into little pieces as you go. Cook until golden and bubbling: about 10 minutes. Scatter torn basil leaves over the top and serve.

Gratin Dauphinois

The ultimate potato dish. It's so good that
I'm quite happy to have this as a main course,
although it also works very well as an
accompaniment to meat, fish or green vegetables.

Preparation: 30 minutes
Cooking: 1 hour 45 minutes

Serves 6

1kg potatoes, such as King Edwards, Desirée,
Idaho or Maris Piper
1 clove of garlic, crushed and peeled
100g butter
20fl oz single cream
sea salt
freshly ground black pepper
100g Gruyère cheese, grated

Heat the oven to 150°C/gas 2.

Peel the potatoes and slice them finely using
a mandolin or a food processor. Place the potato
slices in a large bowl of cold water and move
them around to get rid of excess starch. Drain
well and dry thoroughly: use a salad spinner or
else put the slices in a tea towel, gather the
corners together, go outside and swing your arm
as fast and vigorously as you can …

Rub a large shallow ovenproof dish with the
garlic clove and a little butter.

Put the remaining butter with the cream in a
large saucepan and bring just to the boil. Finely
dice what's left of the garlic and add it to the
butter and cream, along with seasoning and the
potato slices. Gently simmer for 8 minutes.

Transfer to the prepared dish, spread out
evenly and top with the Gruyère and a little more
seasoning. Bake for 1½ hours. Serve hot.

Gratin Dauphinois has everything you need in a main course: a creamy, satisfying texture, lots of flavour and a golden, crispy surface. The story I heard was that it was created for the *dauphin* – the young prince soon to become Henri II – to encourage him to eat his vegetables.

Gratin Dauphinois is well worth the preparation it
takes. Slice the potatoes on a mandolin (you can
buy these very reasonably), then rinse the slices
in fresh water to get rid of starch. Dry them in a
salad spinner or a tea towel. The rest is easy, but
do not rush the cooking. The result is perfection.

Boulangère Potatoes

This dish takes time; don't rush it! The result is worth it: meltingly tender potato slivers topped with a crunchy, golden crust like French bread, hence the name, *Pommes Boulangère*.

Preparation: 25 minutes
Cooking: 90 minutes

Serves 6

1kg floury potatoes, such as Maris Piper, Desirée, King Edwards or Idaho
2 onions
25g butter
300ml hot chicken or vegetable stock
sea salt
freshly ground black pepper
a few sprigs of thyme

Heat the oven to 180°C/gas 4.

Peel the potatoes and slice them very finely using a mandolin or a food processor. Slice the onions in the same way.

Butter an ovenproof dish and make layers of the potatoes and onions, with seasoning and the thyme leaves (stripped from the stalks) sprinkled over each. Finish with a layer of potatoes and try to make a neat overlapping pattern with them. Using the flat of your hand, press down the potatoes firmly.

Pour in the hot stock. Cut the remaining butter into little pieces and dot the top with them. Cover with tin foil and cook for 1 hour.

Remove the foil and bake for a further 30 minutes. The potato should be soft all the way through and the top layer golden brown.

Nutmeg Mash

Proper mash is one of life's small but significant delights. Having tasted this, I just can't understand the packet stuff at all …

Preparation: 10 minutes
Cooking: 30 minutes

Serves 6

1.5kg floury potatoes, such as Maris Piper, Desirée, King Edwards or Idaho
175g butter
300ml milk
1 egg
1/4 tsp freshly grated nutmeg
sea salt
freshly ground black pepper

Peel the potatoes, cut into pieces, place in a saucepan of boiling water and simmer for 20 minutes. Drain well, return to the pan over a low heat and, shaking the pan, allow the excess moisture to steam off. Mash the potatoes until smooth – for perfect mash try using a hand-held ricer.

Place the butter and milk in a saucepan over a medium heat and gently bring to the boil. Slowly pour the melted butter and hot milk into the potatoes, mixing well with a rubber spatula. Break in the egg and beat. Finally, add the nutmeg and seasoning. Mix well, taste and adjust to your personal choice. Serve at once.

Sauté Potatoes

Pommes de Terre Sautées are an excellent accompaniment to roast meat or fish, although I think they are good enough to eat as a main course with a crunchy green salad.

Preparation: 10 minutes
Cooking: 30 minutes

Serves 6

2kg floury potatoes, such as Maris Piper, Desirée, King Edwards or Idaho
8 tbsp olive oil
sea salt
freshly ground black pepper

Peel the potatoes and cook whole in gently boiling water for 12 minutes. Drain and slice into 1cm rounds. Heat the oven to 180°C/gas 4.

Divide the oil between two big frying pans and heat. Place a layer of potatoes over the base of each pan and cook for 5 minutes on each side until golden.

Remove with a slotted spoon and place in a roasting tray with a crumpled up piece of baking parchment in the bottom (this prevents the potatoes on the bottom from going soggy). Keep warm in the hot oven. Repeat until all the potatoes are cooked.

Sprinkle with sea salt and black pepper, and serve at once.

Roasted Asparagus Spears

This is a simple and delicious way to prepare asparagus, and works wonderfully in salads.

Preparation: 10 minutes
Cooking: 10 minutes

Serves 6

500g green asparagus spears
3 tbsp olive oil
sea salt
freshly ground black pepper
juice of 1 lemon
a dash of balsamic vinegar
100g Parmesan cheese

Trim the white ends from the asparagus; I sometimes like to cut at an angle.

Heat the oven to 200°C/gas 6.

Drizzle a large non-stick baking tray with the olive oil, add the asparagus, toss them in the oil, then roast them for 10 minutes. The asparagus around the edge of the tray may be better roasted, so cook the middle pieces for a few minutes longer if needed.

Transfer the roasted asparagus to a serving dish and add seasoning, lemon juice and balsamic vinegar. With a vegetable peeler, carve ribbons of Parmesan over the top. Serve hot or at room temperature.

Snap up fresh green asparagus in season and prepare this wonderful – and wonderfully easy – dish. Eat the asparagus either soon after roasting, while still hot, or save to eat at room temperature later in the day: on a picnic, perhaps.

Green Beans with Pine Nuts

At my grandparents' house I remember throwing closed pinecones into the open fire to make the pine nuts pop out ready-toasted – this has the advantage of being alarming to adults and potentially hazardous, and is therefore tremendous fun. Nowadays you can buy pine nuts in packets at the supermarket, which is less fun, but much easier. These green beans are great served with roast lamb, or added to lightly cooked pasta with chopped tomato and a squeeze of lemon.

Preparation: 10 minutes
Cooking: 8 minutes

Serves 6

400g fine green beans, topped and tailed
50g pine nuts
25g butter
3 tbsp white wine

Plunge the beans into boiling water and cook for 2 minutes.

Heat a non-stick frying pan, and dry-fry the pine nuts – vigilantly – until golden brown. Take care: nothing seems to happen, then suddenly the pine nuts colour.

Drain the beans well and place in a pan with the butter and white wine. Cover and cook for a further minute, add the toasted pine nuts, toss and serve.

Courgettes with Lemon Butter

My grandfather used to grow giant (and quite inedible) marrows in his garden, living by the rule that the bigger they got, the better they were. These baby marrows, however, are at their most sweet and tender, and make an excellent accompaniment to fish or vegetable dishes.

Preparation: 10 minutes
Cooking: 10 minutes

Serves 6

40g butter
2 tbsp olive oil
6 medium courgettes
zest and juice of 1 lemon
sea salt
freshly ground black pepper

Place the butter and oil in a large frying pan and gently heat. Cut the courgettes at an angle into slices about 2.5cm thick. Increase the heat under the oil and melted butter and add a layer of the sliced courgettes, frying them on each side until golden. Remove and keep warm, and repeat until all the courgettes are cooked. Return the courgettes to the pan, add the lemon zest and juice and the seasoning, toss and serve at once.

Ratatouille can be as simple or as complicated as
you want to make it. The main rule is that the longer
you cook it, the better it becomes. So, as with all
casseroles, make it a day in advance to allow
the flavours to merge.

Ratatouille

For variations, try using red wine instead of water, or chillies for extra bite. This is very good with Anouchka's Chilli Garlic Bread (page 61).

Preparation: 30 minutes
Cooking: 1 hour 10 minutes

Serves 6

9 tbsp olive oil
2 red onions, chopped
2 cloves of garlic, crushed, peeled and chopped
3 red peppers, deseeded and roughly chopped
2 aubergines, roughly chopped
4 courgettes, roughly chopped
3 x 410g tins chopped tomatoes, or 1kg fresh tomatoes, skinned
400ml water
a bunch of oregano, chopped
a bunch of marjoram, chopped
a bunch of flat-leaf parsley, chopped
sea salt
freshly ground black pepper

Heat 3 tablespoons of the olive oil in a large saucepan over a medium heat, add the onions and garlic and sauté for 3 minutes. Add the peppers, aubergines and courgettes, mix well and cook for a further 5 minutes or until the vegetables have gained a little colour. Then add the tomatoes, water, herbs and seasoning, mix well and simmer gently over a reduced heat for a further hour, stirring from time to time. When cooked stir in another 6 tablespoons of olive oil and check the seasoning. Serve hot or at room temperature.

Spiced Red Cabbage

This wonderfully comforting dish for autumn and winter is filled with rich, sweet flavours. Best made a day ahead and reheated, it works very well with baked ham, duck or even roast chicken, although I am happy to eat it on its own.

Preparation: 30 minutes
Cooking: 1 hour 15 minutes

Serves 6

50g butter
1 tbsp olive oil
1 small red cabbage, finely sliced
1 red onion, finely sliced
1 red chilli, finely sliced (seeds included if you like the heat)
100ml red wine vinegar or 50ml balsamic
75g unrefined brown sugar
1/2 tsp allspice
1/2 tsp ground cloves
sea salt
freshly ground black pepper
200ml water

Melt the butter with the oil in a saucepan over a medium heat, add the red cabbage, onion and chilli, stir well and cook for 10 minutes. Add the vinegar, sugar, allspice, cloves, seasoning and water, mix well and bring to the boil. Reduce the heat, cover and simmer the dish for 1 hour, checking frequently. If the mixture becomes dry during cooking, add a little more water. Serve hot or reheated.

Roast Vegetables with Couscous

I'm a great fan of couscous, which I use with all kinds of ingredients as an alternative to rice or pasta. It's ridiculously quick and easy to make, healthy, delicious, and has the capacity to soak up flavours, making it extremely versatile. This is a vegetarian version, which can be enjoyed entirely on its own, or as an accompaniment to a meat or fish dish, or with a salad. Try it with a handful of raisins and chopped apricots, and plenty of chopped fresh mint.

Preparation: 30 minutes
Cooking: 40 minutes

Serves 6

4 tbsp olive oil, plus a little extra to serve
2 onions, peeled and cut into wedges
2 shallots, peeled
3 carrots, cut into chunks
2 parsnips, cut into chunks
3 cloves of garlic, crushed, peeled and chopped
1 red chilli, finely sliced (seeds included if you like the heat)
1 tsp paprika
1/2 tsp ground cinnamon
1/2 tsp coriander seeds, crushed
1/2 tsp cumin seeds, crushed
4 cardamom pods, crushed
large pinch of saffron
2 courgettes, thickly sliced
500g plum tomatoes, skinned
sea salt
freshly ground black pepper
450g couscous
75g butter
a bunch of flat-leaf parsley, chopped
a bunch of coriander, chopped
a dash of balsamic vinegar

Heat the oven to 190°C/gas 5.

Heat the olive oil in a large, heavy-based roasting tin directly over a medium heat. Add the onions, shallots, carrots and parsnips and cook for about 10 minutes until golden, stirring frequently. Add the garlic, chilli, paprika, cinnamon, coriander, cumin and cardamom and stir well, coating the vegetables in all the spices. Cook for a further 4 minutes then remove from the heat and stir in the saffron, courgettes, tomatoes and seasoning. Transfer to the oven to roast for 40 minutes. Check after 30 minutes, adding a little water or vegetable stock if desired.

Place the couscous in a large bowl and cover with boiling water to a level of 2.5cm above the grains. Mix well and leave to stand for 5 minutes. Meanwhile, melt the butter in a small saucepan, add the chopped herbs and cook for 1 minute. Pour over the couscous, mix well and season it.

Take the vegetables out of the oven, drizzle with olive oil and balsamic vinegar, and serve with the couscous.

My daughter loves making these crisp roasted peppers, and designing new fillings for them. Try them with rice, or couscous with dried fruit, or slices of pancetta – the variations are endless.

Baked Red Peppers

Use good, well-ripened red peppers for a
cheery, colourful summer dish.

Preparation: 25 minutes
Cooking: 1 hour 25 minutes

Serves 6

3 red peppers
olive oil
1 large red onion, peeled and cut into wedges
1 medium fennel bulb, trimmed and cut
into wedges
3 cloves of garlic, crushed, peeled and sliced
sea salt
freshly ground black pepper
200g goat's cheese

Heat the oven to 120°C/gas ½.
Cut the peppers in half and remove and discard
the entire core. Lightly oil a baking tray and place
the peppers on it.

Put the onion, fennel and garlic in a bowl,
drizzle over some olive oil and add seasoning.
Mix to coat the vegetables in oil and seasoning,
and then divide them among the peppers,
stuffing them inside the pepper halves. Bake for
1 hour 20 minutes.

Remove the stuffed peppers from the oven
and increase the heat to 190°C/gas 5. Slice the
goat's cheese and arrange it over the peppers.
Return the tray to the oven and roast for
5 minutes, until the cheese is bubbling.

Desserts

The names of French desserts are a translator's nightmare: *le gâteau* is a generic term for 'cake', although perplexingly, *le cake* refers to a kind of tea bread. The word *tarte* covers a wide variety of recipes, from the open fruit tarts to the upside-down Tarte Tatin, but there is no true word for 'pie' – unless we count *tourte*, which is most often used as a term of abuse. And as for translating some of the bizarre names of the confections to be found in French *pâtisseries* – it is almost impossible. Many of them are religious in origin – Saint-Honoré has a cake named after him, filled with whipped cream and sugar.

But the French have a long-standing tradition of irreverence towards the Catholic Church which extends even into the kitchen. How else can we explain the *religieuse* – that little cake made up of two choux buns one on top of the other, so that it looks like a fat little nun? Or even the deliciously named *pet de nonne*? These small, chocolate-coated pastries are now served under a respectable alias in some of our more elegant restaurants, but the original name – still gleefully used in many regions of France – translates as 'the nun's fart'. Remember that, next time you eat a profiterole.

It is a peculiar fact that the French, who make
the most wonderful cakes, rarely eat dessert on a
day-to-day basis. Fruit, yoghurt and cheese are the
most usual endings to a meal, but on Sundays and
during special celebrations, desserts really come
into their own.

Blueberry Tart

Blueberries are plump, cultivated berries, which develop a great taste when cooked. Bilberries are tiny and grow wild in Europe, and have a sharp, tart flavour. The two are sometimes confused because of the similarity of the names. I like to make this tart with bilberries – *Tarte aux Myrtilles* – which are hard to find but worth it (this is the only thing that motivates me to brave the moors and pick a batch once in a while), but you can use any berry fruit in season; and besides blueberries, which the tart shown here is made from, blackberries, raspberries, blackcurrants and tayberries all work well. The *pâte brisée* is crumbly and light, like freshly baked biscuit, and although it is very easy to prepare, this is the kind of dessert that always gives me a sense of achievement.

Preparation: 40 minutes plus 1 hour's chilling
Cooking: 35 minutes

Serves 6

For the *pâte brisée*:
250g flour
175g butter, cut into small knobs, plus extra for greasing
20g unrefined caster sugar
1 egg
$1/2$ tbsp water

For the filling:
500g blueberries or other berries, stalks removed
2 eggs
125g unrefined caster sugar, plus extra for sprinkling
175ml double cream
25g flour
1 dessertspoonful *crème de cassis*

Rub the flour and butter together with your fingertips until the mixture looks like breadcrumbs. It really helps to work in a cool kitchen and have cool fingers. Mix in the sugar. Then add the egg and water, using a round-ended knife in a cutting motion to combine the ingredients until they form into a pastry ball. Put the pastry ball on to a cool, floured work surface and lightly knead with the palm of your hand for a minute, to ensure a smooth pastry. Wrap and place in the fridge to rest for 40 minutes.

Lightly butter a 25cm push-up-bottom flan tin. Dust a cool surface with flour and roll out the chilled pastry to more than fit the tin (because you do not want to have to stretch it). As this is a high-butter-content pastry, take care not to let the pastry stick to the surface – keep dusting lightly with flour. Line the tin with the rolled-out pastry with the excess lying over the edges, and to trim it, simply roll the pin over the flan tin. Return the pastry to the fridge for 20 minutes.

Heat the oven to 200°C/gas 6.

Place the berries in the chilled pastry case. Mix together the eggs, sugar, cream, flour and cassis until smooth and pour over the fruit. Lightly sprinkle with a little extra sugar and bake for 35 minutes. Serve cold, if you can wait.

You find fruit tarts like this one in all the most elegant *pâtisseries* in France; my mother used to buy them for birthdays and saint's days, but they are far too good to be kept for special occasions.

Strawberry Tart

This spectacular tart, *Tarte aux Fraises*, can also be made with any other fresh fruit – try raspberries, gages, peaches or apricots – and it looks terrific every time. These desserts were what I always had on festival days as a child, and their jewel colours and wonderful textures and scents will give an instant carnival atmosphere to any table. These tarts don't keep well, so eat on the same day: though who could not? Serve with thick cream.

Preparation: 40 minutes plus 1 hour's chilling
Cooking: 45 minutes

Serves 6

For the almond pastry:
225g flour
75g ground almonds
200g butter, cut into small knobs,
plus extra for greasing
150g unrefined light brown sugar
2–3 egg yolks

For the filling:
200g redcurrant jelly
1kg strawberries

Mix together the flour and ground almonds. Rub the butter into the flour with your fingertips until it resembles breadcrumbs. (Remember: cool kitchen and cool fingers, if you can.) Mix in the sugar. Then add the egg yolks and mix them in using a round-ended knife in a cutting motion until the ingredients come together into a pastry ball. Put the pastry ball on to a cool, floured work surface and lightly knead with the palm of your hand for a minute, to ensure a smooth pastry. Wrap and place in the fridge to rest for 40 minutes.

Lightly butter a 25cm push-up-bottom flan tin. Roll out the pastry on a lightly floured surface, then line the tin. Place in the fridge to chill again for 20 minutes.

Heat the oven to 180°C/gas 4.

Line the pastry case with baking parchment and baking beans and bake for 20 minutes. Then remove the lining paper and beans, reduce the heat to 150°C/gas 2, and bake for a further 25 minutes until the pastry is golden and set. Remove from the oven and allow to cool.

Gently heat the redcurrant jelly in a small saucepan over a low heat until thin and smooth. Allow the jelly to cool a little.

Carefully release the cooled pastry case and transfer it to a large flat plate. Do take care, as this pastry is fragile. Cut any large strawberries into smaller pieces, then pile the fruit into the case. Spoon the redcurrant jelly over the strawberries to give an even coating, leave to set for 1 hour, then serve.

Lemon Tart

This is my great-aunt Simone's version of an old and well-loved dish, *Tarte au Citron*. I love it: the creamy filling has an intense, sunny flavour, and I like it best in winter, when I eat it to counteract seasonal blues. It's one of Anouchka's favourite desserts, too, and it's easy enough to make that she can help me. I have to watch her carefully, though – she eats the lemons when I'm not looking!

Preparation: 40 minutes plus 1 hour's chilling
Cooking: 35 minutes

Serves 6

For the *pâte brisée*:
250g flour
175g butter, cut into small knobs
20g unrefined caster sugar
1 egg
2 tsp water

For the filling:
2 eggs
100g unrefined sugar
150ml double cream
zest and juice of 2 lemons
50g butter

Rub the flour and butter together with your fingertips until the mixture looks like breadcrumbs. (A cool kitchen and cool fingers help.) Mix in the sugar. Add the egg and water and mix it in using a round-ended knife in a cutting motion until the ingredients come together into a dough ball.

Put the pastry ball on to a cool, floured work surface and lightly knead with the palm of your hand for a minute, to ensure a smooth pastry. Wrap and place in the fridge to rest for 40 minutes.

Lightly butter a 25cm push-up-bottom flan tin. Roll out the pastry on a lightly floured surface, then line the tin. Trim the edges with a knife and return to the fridge for 20 minutes to chill and relax.

Heat the oven to 180°C/gas 4.

Put the eggs, sugar, double cream and lemon zest and juice into a bowl and whisk well until creamy. Melt the butter and whisk it into the lemon mixture, then pour it into the chilled pastry case.

Carefully place the tart in the oven and bake for 15 minutes, then reduce the heat to 160°C/gas 3 and bake for a further 20 minutes or until the filling has set. Leave to cool for 1 hour before serving.

Grandmother's Festival Loaf

This is a lovely loaf, half bread, half cake, traditionally from the Auvergne region, hence its name: *Fouace Aveyronnaise.*

Preparation: 30 minutes, plus 2 hours' proving
Cooking: 30 minutes

Serves 6

120ml milk
7g yeast and a pinch of sugar
375g flour
50g butter, softened
1 tbsp orange flower water or rum
40g unrefined sugar
2 eggs, plus 1 egg, beaten, for glazing
100g crystallized fruits, chopped

Barely warm the milk, just to remove the chill, then sprinkle in the yeast and sugar and leave to sit for a few minutes.

Place the flour, butter, orange flower water or rum, sugar, eggs and yeast-and-milk mixture in a large bowl and mix well. Add the crystallized fruit and then turn the dough out on to a lightly floured surface. Knead for 8 minutes.

Return the dough to the bowl, cover, and keep in a warm place for 1 hour. The mixture should double in size.

Turn out the dough on to a floured surface again and knead until the dough is soft and elastic. Lightly butter a baking sheet and dust it with flour. Shape the dough into a long sausage, join the two ends together into a circle, place it on the baking tray, glaze with egg and leave it to rest for 1 hour.

Heat the oven to 200°C/gas 6. Just before placing the loaf in the oven glaze it with egg again. Cook for 30 minutes until golden brown.

I find bread-making extremely therapeutic, and this finished loaf looks beautiful, like a summer garland studded with colourful pieces of crystallized fruit. I like to make it on Midsummer's Eve, and eat it out in the garden with cheese, fruit and honey.

Breton Flan

This typical Breton flan, *Far Breton*, is a favourite emergency dessert, and all the members of my family have a different version of it. This one belongs to Juliette Jeuland of Châteaubourg, and uses the traditional prunes, but you can also use dried apricots, cherries, berries or raisins soaked in Armagnac.

Preparation: 10 minutes
Cooking: 30 minutes

Serves 6

3 eggs
100g unrefined light brown sugar, plus extra for dusting
125g flour
500ml milk
80g butter, plus extra for greasing
150g pitted prunes

Heat the oven to 180°C/gas 4.

Mix together the eggs, sugar and flour in a bowl until smooth and blended.

Warm the milk and butter until the butter has melted, then add to the flour mixture and blend together well. Finally, stir in the prunes.

Butter a low-sided earthenware dish and pour the prune mixture into it. Cook for 30 minutes, until risen and browned on top. Dust with sugar, and serve warm or cold.

Gâteau Breton

This is a traditional Breton cake with a rich, buttery taste and a slightly 'sandy' texture, like that of the *sablé* biscuits of the region. Everyone has their own private way of doing it. This is the plain recipe, from Danielle Stéphan of Trégastel, but you can fill your gâteau with raspberry jam, prunes or liqueur-soaked fruit for a moist, luxurious version.

Preparation: 30 minutes
Cooking: 35 minutes

Serves 6

200g flour
50g soft butter, cut into small knobs, plus extra for greasing
200g unrefined caster sugar
zest of 1 orange
5 egg yolks
milk for glazing

Heat the oven to 160°C/gas 3. Generously butter a 24cm push-up-bottom cake tin.

Place the flour in a bowl, add the butter, sugar, orange zest and egg yolks, and work together with your fingers until all the ingredients are evenly blended – the mixture will be quite sticky. Put the mixture into the prepared cake tin and spread it out with your hands.

Make a pattern in the top of the cake mixture with a knife or pastry cutter, and brush the surface with a little milk. Bake for 35 minutes, until the cake is golden brown and has come away from the sides of the tin.

Leave to cool in the tin for 5 minutes before turning out.

Tarte Tatin

This beautifully golden, caramelized tart is best served warm, but not too hot, so that the flavours really get the chance to develop. It is a wonderful autumn recipe for home-grown apples, such as Cox's Orange Pippins – or Bramley's, if you prefer something with a little more bite.

Preparation: 35 minutes plus 30 minutes' chilling
Cooking: 55 minutes

Serves 6

For the pastry:
150g flour, plus extra for dusting
100g butter, cut into small knobs
25g unrefined caster sugar
2 egg yolks

For the apples:
100g unrefined caster sugar
40g butter
5 eating apples, peeled, cored and quartered

To make the pastry, rub together the flour and butter with your fingertips until it resembles breadcrumbs. Mix in the sugar.

Add the egg yolks and, with a round-bladed knife, use a cutting motion to mix until the breadcrumbs gather together to form a ball. Turn the pastry ball out on to a floured surface, dust your hands with a little flour and knead the pastry together until smooth.

Wrap and chill in the fridge for 30 minutes. Place a 20–25cm ovenproof frying pan over a medium heat, and melt the butter and sugar until syrupy.

Heat the oven to 200°C/gas 6.

Arrange the apple quarters in the frying pan and cook for 15 minutes: this gives the golden colour to the apples and allows the sugar to turn to caramel.

Roll out the pastry on a lightly floured surface to a size slightly greater than the frying pan. Remove the frying pan from the heat and quickly lay the pastry over the apples, tucking in any excess around the edges. Place in the oven and cook for 20 minutes, then reduce the heat to 160°C/gas 3 and cook for a further 20 minutes.

Remove from the oven and gently ease a knife all the way around the edge of the tart. Place a large heatproof plate upside down on top of the frying pan and quickly turn over the pan and plate, releasing the tart on to the plate. Lift off the frying pan to reveal golden brown apples and a syrupy sauce.

Hot puddings are a rarity in France, but this famous
tart is one of the best. I particularly like it when it is
very slightly burnt, so that the caramel develops a
smoky flavour and the pastry a sticky, crispy texture.
Perfect with good vanilla ice-cream.

Apple Slipper

This little flaky butter pastry, *Chausson aux Pommes*, is named for its shape. It is a favourite with children at *goûter*, the four o'clock snack that is traditional in France. Serve it warm.

Preparation: 2 hours plus 1 hour's chilling
Cooking: 1 hour

Serves 6

250g cold butter
250g flour, plus extra for dusting
75ml cold water
500g apples, peeled, cored and diced
25g unrefined caster sugar, plus extra for dusting
1/2 tsp cinnamon
1 beaten egg for sealing

Take 200g of the butter, hard from the fridge, and cut it into very small pieces. Place the pieces on a tray and leave to soften for 20 minutes.

Put the flour in a bowl, add a few pieces of butter and toss them in the flour using a round-bladed knife. Continue adding butter until all of it is well coated in flour, so that no pieces get the chance to clump together. Add the cold water and with a cutting motion quickly mix until the pastry comes together into a ball.

Transfer to a lightly dusted, cool surface and gently shape with your hands into a brick. Roll out to an oblong about 18 x 10cm. Fold one third over to the centre, the other third over that, then use the rolling pin to press the edges together, trapping pockets of air. Let it rest for 5 minutes.

Lightly flour the surface again, give the pastry a quarter turn, and repeat as above. Do this three more times. Wrap and chill for 1 hour.

Melt the remaining 50g butter in a large frying pan over a moderate heat, add the apples and cook gently for 5 minutes. Stir in the sugar and cinnamon, remove from the heat and allow to cool completely.

Heat the oven to 190°C/gas 5.

Dust a baking sheet with flour and roll out the pastry to a circle about 1cm thick. Spoon the apples into one half, brush the edges with egg and fold the pastry over into a half-moon shape. Crimp the edges with your fingers to seal them. Brush with egg , pierce with a fork and dust with sugar. Bake for 20 minutes. Reduce the heat to 160°F/gas 3 and bake for 20 minutes more.

Cherry Clafoutis

This simple pudding can also be made with other soft fruits, such as apricots, plums, peaches, blackberries and blackcurrants.

Preparation: 40 minutes
Cooking: 1 hour 10 minutes

Serves 6

15g butter for greasing
750g cherries, pitted
125g flour
50g unrefined caster sugar
3 eggs
1 tsp vanilla extract
300ml milk
unrefined icing sugar for dusting

Heat the oven to 180°C/gas 4. Butter a shallow ovenproof dish. Place the cherries in the dish.

Put the flour and sugar in a large bowl and make a well in the middle. Whisk the eggs; add the vanilla and milk to the eggs and whisk. Slowly pour the milk mix into the flour, beating constantly until all the liquid has been added and you have a smooth batter. Pour over the cherries.

Bake for 40 minutes until the batter is firm to the touch and golden on top. Sprinkle with icing sugar and serve just warm.

This is a summer favourite with children – although
the grown-up version, with the addition of kirsch,
also goes down rather well. I got this recipe from
my aunt Claudine, whose cherry trees I remember
with great affection.

Braised Cherries with Spiced Toasts

The French name is *Soupe aux Cerises*, though this is not quite what we expect from a soup.

Preparation: 40 minutes
Cooking: 20 minutes

Serves 6

500g black cherries, pitted
2 tbsp unrefined sugar
1 tbsp kirsch (for adults)
75g butter
10 slices of baguette
50g unrefined sugar
1 tsp cinnamon
1/2 tbsp flour

Place the cherries, sugar and kirsch in a saucepan over a medium heat. Bring to the boil, then reduce the heat and simmer for 15 minutes.

Heat the butter in a frying pan and fry the slices of baguette on each side until golden.

Remove the bread, dust with sugar and cinnamon, and place at the bottom of a serving dish. When the cherries are soft and cooked, remove them from the juice and pile on to the bread.

Blend the flour with a little water and, using a balloon whisk, quickly mix this into the warm cherry juice. Gently bring to the boil. The mixture will thicken slightly, becoming velvety. Pour over the bread and cherries, and serve.

Chantilly Meringues

These light and fluffy meringues are perfect with fruit, such as a bowl of fresh summer berries, or the Slow Fudge Sauce on this page, or a drizzle of chocolate fondue (page 233): or perhaps more than one of these …

Preparation: 15 minutes
Cooking: 2 hours (or more)

Serves 6

For the meringues:
3 egg whites
180g unrefined caster sugar

For the crème Chantilly:
300ml double cream
25g unrefined caster sugar
few drops vanilla extract

Heat the oven to 140°C/gas 1.
Place the egg whites in a mixing bowl and beat with an electric whisk until stiff. (Or whisk by hand … until stiff.) Beat in half the sugar, then add the remaining sugar and beat.

Line a baking tray with baking parchment and scoop the meringue mixture on to the paper in 12 spoonfuls. Bake for 2 hours. For perfect crisp and dry meringues, turn the oven off but leave the meringues to cool in there for a further 12 hours.

Whisk the cream with the sugar and vanilla extract until it stands in soft peaks. Scoop cream on to 6 of the meringues, then sandwich the other 6 meringues on top of these. Chill before serving.

Slow Fudge Sauce

This tantalizingly slow fudge sauce – Caramel Marie Sorin, from my great-aunt Marinette – is a luxury for those days when ice cream alone just isn't enough. Part of the pleasure of this recipe is the time it takes to prepare it and the anticipation that goes with it. By the time it is ready, the entire house smells like a sweet shop, spirits have magically lifted and even the rain has stopped. If you have some left (this has never happened to me yet), then line a tin with baking paper, pour in the sauce and leave it to set in the fridge for a couple of hours. Then cut into squares for a smooth and creamy fudge.

Preparation: 5 minutes
Cooking: 30 minutes

Serves 6

500g unrefined sugar
10g butter
400g tin condensed milk
75ml milk

Put all the ingredients in a heavy-based pan and cook over a very low heat, stirring constantly until all the sugar has melted. You must stir constantly, otherwise the sugar will burn and the sauce becomes inedible. Slowly bring to the boil, and simmer very gently for 20 minutes, continuing to stir all the while.

Remove from the heat and beat well with a wooden spoon. Serve warm with a really good vanilla ice cream.

Crème Brûlée

This is a quick and easy version of a perennial favourite – try adding a handful of redcurrants or raspberries to the mixture for a fresh, summery variation. Make this a day before serving it to get a really firm set.

Preparation: 15 minutes, plus overnight chilling
Cooking: 20 minutes

Serves 6

1 vanilla pod
375ml double cream
5 egg yolks
25g unrefined caster sugar
unrefined icing sugar, to serve

Cut the vanilla pod in half lengthways, scrape out the seeds and put them in a small saucepan with the cream. Discard the pod. Gently bring the cream to a simmer – do not boil – then remove from the heat.

Heat the oven to 160°C/gas 3.

In a bowl, beat together the egg yolks and caster sugar until light and fluffy. Stir in the warmed cream and mix well.

Make a bain-marie. Place the mixing bowl over a saucepan of simmering water on a gentle heat, stirring constantly until the mixture coats the back of the spoon: about 8 minutes.

Pour the custard into individual ramekins (or you could use one large ovenproof serving dish).

Make a bain-marie with a deep roasting tin: place the dishes in the tin and half-fill the tin with hot water. Place it in the oven and cook the custards for 20 minutes. Remove and allow to cool, then place in the fridge overnight.

The next day, heat the grill to high. Sieve the icing sugar over the custards and place under the grill. The sugar will melt and caramelize. Move the dishes around so that they brown evenly. Leave to cool completely before serving.

Crème Caramel

This is one of my favourite desserts. No two people make it in exactly the same way, but this is my grandmother's recipe, and ideally it should be made 24 hours in advance to give the rich caramel colour at the bottom of the dish time to develop.

Preparation: 20 minutes, plus 1 hour or overnight chilling
Cooking: 1 hour

Serves 6

For the caramel:
200g unrefined caster sugar
50ml water

For the cream:
500ml milk
3 eggs
2 egg yolks
60g unrefined sugar
a few drops of vanilla extract

Heat the oven to 160°C/gas 3. Place an ovenproof soufflé dish in the oven to warm.

Make the caramel. Place the sugar and water in a small pan. Bring to the boil, then simmer until golden brown. Pour into the warm soufflé dish.

Place the milk in a pan and bring gently to the boil. Take off the heat.

Mix together the eggs, egg yolks, sugar and vanilla extract in a bowl. Pour this into the hot milk and stir well. Strain the mixture through a fine sieve into the caramel-lined soufflé dish.

Make a bain-marie: place the dish in a deep roasting tin and half-fill the tin with hot water. Carefully place in the oven and cook for 1 hour. Remove and allow to cool, then place in the fridge for an hour before serving (or overnight).

To turn out the caramel, run a knife around the custard. Place a deep-sided serving plate over the top and invert the dish into the plate. Carefully remove the soufflé dish, and serve.

Kirsch Soufflé

Soufflé means 'blown', like glass, and people tend to think that soufflés are delicate and tricky to make. This isn't true; it's a quick, light, versatile dish – just avoid opening the oven door while your soufflé is cooking, and eat it straight away once cooked. This shouldn't be a problem – it's irresistible!

Preparation: 20 minutes
Cooking: 15 minutes

Serves 6

butter for greasing
2 tbsp unrefined caster sugar
50g flour
200ml milk
75g unrefined sugar
20g butter
4 egg yolks
125ml kirsch
7 egg whites

Heat the oven to 190°C/gas 5.

Take a 20cm soufflé dish – or 6 individual ramekins – and lightly rub with a little butter, then coat with a layer of sugar. Roll the dish(es) around until evenly coated with the sugar.

Place the flour in a bowl, add a little milk and work to form a smooth paste.

Heat the remaining milk, sugar and butter in a saucepan. When this reaches the boil, slowly pour it into the flour paste, whisking with a balloon whisk until the mixture is smooth. Return the mixture to the pan and bring to the boil, stirring constantly. Remove from the heat and add the egg yolks and kirsch, mixing well until smooth.

Beat the egg whites in a large bowl with an electric whisk until stiff. Add the kirsch mixture to the whites and fold in quickly until evenly blended. Carefully pour into the prepared soufflé dish or dishes, put immediately into the oven and cook for 10 minutes.

Without removing the soufflé from the oven, dust with icing sugar and cook for a further 5 minutes. Serve immediately on warmed plates.

There are plenty of variations for this easy dish – try using Grand Marnier, chartreuse or rum for a change, and serve with a sweet, fruity wine such as Sauternes or Monbazillac.

Ripe pears just off the tree have almost nothing in common with the hard, green ones you find in some supermarkets. Choose a firm, slightly floury species (such as Williams), which will really absorb the flavours of the wine and spices.

Pears Poached in Red Wine

Poires au Vin Rouge is a terrific way of preparing autumn pears, and fills the house with a marvellous scent of wine and spices. The juice makes a wonderful spicy punch – just add a little cognac!

Preparation: 25 minutes
Cooking: 30 minutes

Serves 6

1 bottle red Burgundy
4 cloves
2 blades of mace
100g unrefined caster sugar
6 pears

Place the red wine, cloves, mace and caster sugar in a saucepan (large enough also to accommodate the pears) and gently bring to a simmer.

Peel the pears, carefully keeping their beautiful shape and the stem on. Add the pears to the wine and simmer for 30 minutes, turning the pears to ensure even cooking and staining from the red wine.

Leave the pears to cool in the wine and then serve at room temperature. The pears can be served on their own or in a soup bowl with a ladleful of the red wine.

Pear and Chocolate Brioche Pudding

Brioche is a lovely soft roll or loaf made from a yeast dough enriched with eggs and butter, which give it its distinctive colour and flavour. Brioche varies in shape from region to region, with the Parisian variety – a small ball of brioche on top of a larger base, or *brioche à tête* – perhaps most familiar to us. The most highly regarded brioches come from Gournay and Gisors in Normandy. Serve with scoops of real vanilla ice cream for a melt-in-your-mouth pudding.

Preparation: 25 minutes plus 40 minutes' resting
Cooking: 45 minutes

Serves 6

butter for greasing
300g brioche, sliced
5 ripe pears, peeled and sliced
450ml cream
450ml milk
100g chocolate (70 per cent cocoa)
50g unrefined caster sugar, plus extra for sprinkling
3 eggs

Butter a low-sided ovenproof dish. Arrange the slices of brioche and pear alternately in the dish. Warm the cream and milk in a saucepan over a low heat. Break the chocolate into small pieces, add it to the warm milk and cream along with the sugar, and stir until melted. Do not boil. Whisk the eggs and mix them into the warm chocolatey milk, then pour the liquid over the brioche and pear slices, wetting the entire brioche. Press down with a spatula, and leave to stand for 40 minutes.

Heat the oven to 160°C/gas 3.
Sprinkle the pudding with a little extra sugar, and place it in a bain-marie (that is, place the baking dish in a large roasting tin and fill the tin with hot water to come halfway up the pudding dish).

Place in the oven and cook for 45 minutes until soft and golden.

Polenta Pudding Cake

This warm polenta-based pudding cake, *Gâteau Francesca*, is lovely cold-weather comfort food.

Preparation: 20 minutes
Cooking: 30 minutes

Serves 6

250g butter, plus extra for greasing
250g unrefined caster sugar
3 unwaxed lemons
4 eggs
125g polenta
25g ground almonds
100g flour
cream, to serve

Heat the oven to 160°C/gas 3. Lightly butter a 20cm pie dish.

Cream together the butter and caster sugar with an electric whisk until soft and smooth. Finely grate the lemon zest from two and a half of the lemons and then juice them. Add the zest and juice to the cake mix and blend. Thinly slice the remaining half a lemon and keep on one side.

Beat the eggs into the cake mix —it will split, but do not worry, this is normal. Then beat in the polenta and ground almonds. Finally, fold in the flour with a large spoon.

Transfer the cake mix to the buttered dish, arrange the lemon slices on top and bake for 25–30 minutes. Serve warm, with cream.

Mémée's Cherries

Of all my great-grandmother's recipes, this is the one I remember best. She gave my mother several jars of these preserved cherries when my mother came to England, and there are still some left, a precious few, in a big jar at the bottom of the liqueur cabinet. On special occasions, we drink a little of the liqueur, with a single cherry at the bottom of the glass. The cherries are forty years old now, and they have macerated for so long that even the stones – and the little nut inside – are infused with the flavour of the Armagnac. You can use the same basic recipe for almost any fruit: raspberries, small plums, blackberries, redcurrants. You can vary the alcohol, too; any kind of clear spirit works well, including vodka or white rum. I make my own now, although I still like Mémée's best. Perhaps in another forty years …

Preparation: 30 minutes
Steeping: up to forty years!

Serves 6

sour cherries
Armagnac
unrefined caster sugar
a pinch of cinnamon
you also need a Mason sealable jar

Choose undamaged sour cherries of very good quality. Wash the cherries and leave the stones in. Cut off part of the stem only with scissors.

Put 3 layers of cherries at the bottom of the jar. Top with 2 to 3 tablespoons of caster sugar. Add a pinch of cinnamon. Repeat this process till you are close to the top of the jar, then cover with about 2cm of sugar. Top with spirit so that the fruit is covered. Seal the jar.

Turn the jar a few times to dissolve the sugar. Turn again in a few days' time.

Consume after a few months (the longer you wait, the better the result).

Sloe Gin and Mango Crush

This makes a delicious and wickedly refreshing end to a rich meal.

Preparation: 25 minutes
Freezing: 70 minutes

Serves 6

3 large ripe mangoes
50ml gin
50ml sloe gin
50g dark chocolate (70 per cent cocoa),
cut into small pieces

Place 6 glasses in the freezer.

Peel the skin away from the mango with a sharp knife, then cut all the flesh away from the stone and roughly chop it. Place it in a bowl and blend with a hand-held blender until the mixture is a purée. Add the gin and sloe gin and mix well.

Place in the freezer for 1 hour and then remove and break up the crystals with a fork. Return to the freezer and chill for 10 minutes before again breaking up the crystals with a fork.

Repeat this process at least 5 or 6 times, or until the crystals are firm enough to hold their shape. Fill the chilled glasses with the crush and return it to the fridge for 10 minutes. Serve at once with a small nib of dark chocolate.

My brother came up with this delicious and unusual
dessert – so simple, and yet so good! My daughter
prefers the alcohol-free version, topped with a
cherry and curls of milk chocolate.

Chocolate

I have to admit that for a while after writing *Chocolat* I felt that I would never be able to eat chocolate again. After months of chocolate festivals, chocolate premières, chocolate factories, chocolate-themed parties and openings and dinners, after being on the set of the film, where even the wood shavings smelt of chocolate, I think even the most devoted chocolate addict might have begun to feel rather sated. I was disgusted, chocced-out, finished.

The Italians saved me; as I arrived at yet another chocolate event, this time in the exquisite coffee-shop and *chocolaterie* of Cova, in Milan, I was greeted by the owner, who, taking one look at my pale, exhausted face, smiled and said: 'Wait here. I have something special for you to try.' As he vanished into a back room, I tried to school my features (for the thousandth time) into an expression of blissful surprise: *Chocolate! My favourite!*

I felt my worst suspicions about to be confirmed when the gentleman returned carrying a silver tray – which on closer examination revealed a generous pile of the most incredible, delicious, vocabulary-challengingly excellent anchovy toasts I have ever eaten. I spent that blissful afternoon gorging on anchovy toasts and plump black olives, and when I got home again I found that my chocolate aversion had magically disappeared. I was cured.

As a result, when we were compiling this book we found that the chocolate recipes outnumbered the rest to such an extent that we decided to create an entirely separate section devoted to this uniquely versatile and enchanting substance. Some of the recipes are from *Chocolat* – the ones you keep asking me for – and some are old (or new) favourites gathered along the way.

To my great disappointment, the gentleman from Cova refused to give me the exact recipe for the life-saving anchovy toasts, but you can make a good approximation of it using the tapenade recipe on page 59.

Chocolate: a unique substance. It can be melted, grated, sculpted and spun. It can be eaten in savouries as well as sweets with equal pleasure, or just devoured on its own. Bliss.

Tempering Chocolate

Note for all chocolates-lovers: never store chocolate in the fridge or cool it in the fridge.

Couverture is also called dipping or coating chocolate, and professional chocolate makers always use it. It comes in all varieties, but has a high cocoa butter content, thus making it ideal for hand-made chocolates. The best couverture comes from France, Belgium and Switzerland. Couverture needs to be tempered in order to give it a perfectly smooth and glossy finish.

Tempering is really very simple, and although it takes a little time, it is worth the effort to achieve a really professional gloss. You will need a sugar thermometer, and then all the process requires is to take the couverture to a certain temperature and then to cool it. This changes the crystalline structure of the chocolate and makes it shiny and manageable.

If the idea of tempering chocolate really doesn't appeal, you can simply melt good quality eating chocolate using the bain-marie method. It tastes fine, although your chocolate will not have the shiny, professional texture or the 'snap' of tempered couverture.

To temper chocolate:
First break the chocolate into small pieces. If it comes from a professional supplier it may already come as buttons.

Place the chocolate in a heatproof dish. Make a bain-marie by standing the dish in a pan of simmering water over a low heat, and warm through, stirring occasionally.

Then, when the chocolate reaches 45°C, remove the dish from the bain-marie and stand it in a pan of cold water. Mix well and allow the temperature to drop back to 25°C.

Finally, return the dish to the hot bain-marie, mix well and heat the chocolate to 30°C.

The chocolate has now been tempered and is ready for use.

Mendiants

These are my own favourites – little discs of chocolate sprinkled with whatever you like best: almonds, candied lemon peel, glacé cherries, walnuts or fat Malaga raisins. Anouchka likes to do the artistic part (while I do most of the eating). The name means 'beggars'. Traditionally served at Christmas with toppings of dried fruit and nuts in four colours, they were meant to represent the four Roman Catholic mendicant orders (white for the Dominicans, grey for the Franciscans, brown for the Carmelites and deep purple for the Augustines).

Preparation: 1 hour
Setting: 1 hour

Makes about 65

500g milk or dark couverture, tempered as on page 216
150g of your combined choice of almonds, walnuts, raisins, sultanas, candied fruits

Place teaspoonfuls of the couverture on a large sheet of baking parchment. Gently spread each one with the back of the spoon to make a 2.5cm-diameter circle. Scatter the fruits and nuts on top of the discs and allow to cool.

Apricot Truffles

The slight sharpness of the apricot provides a delicious contrast to the dark chocolate in these luscious truffles.

Preparation: 2 hours
Setting: 1 hour

Makes about 36

450g milk chocolate (70 per cent cocoa)
170ml milk
1 tbsp apricot liqueur
12 soft dried apricots, finely diced
100g milk couverture
200g cocoa powder

Put the chocolate in a heatproof bowl. Place in a bain-marie (over a saucepan of simmering water), and mix until melted. Heat the milk in a small saucepan until boiling. Pour into the melted chocolate and stir well. Add the liqueur and blend until smooth.

Remove from the heat. Gradually add the apricot pieces, stirring constantly. As the mixture cools it will thicken and form a workable paste. Allow to cool so that you can roll the mixture into balls between your fingers. Leave to cool completely, while you temper the couverture for dipping (see page 216).

Sift the cocoa powder on to a plate. Using a thin fork, stab the truffles one at a time, dip in the tempered chocolate, then roll in the cocoa powder and leave to cool.

Left to right are untipped Nipples of Venus, Mendiants, finished Nipples of Venus (see page 220) and Apricot Truffles. For a shortcut version of the truffles, don't bother with the couverture and simply roll the truffles in cocoa powder.

Nipples of Venus

This was originally an Italian confection, but I put it in because I couldn't resist the name ...

Preparation: 2 hours
Setting: 1 hour

Makes about 70

For the filling:
225g dark chocolate (70 per cent cocoa)
300ml double cream

For dipping:
100g dark chocolate (70 per cent cocoa)
50g white chocolate

For the filling, break the chocolate into small pieces and place in a heatproof bowl. Make a bain-marie (put the bowl over a saucepan of simmering water) and allow the chocolate to melt. Heat the cream in a small saucepan and add it to the melted chocolate, mixing until evenly blended. Leave to cool for 2 hours. Then, using an electric whisk, beat until the mixture becomes stiff and holds its shape.

Line 3 baking trays with baking parchment. Put the filling mixture into a piping bag with a 1cm plain nozzle and pipe little mounds – or nipples – on to the baking parchment. Put in the fridge to chill and set.

Melt the dark chocolate in a bain-marie. Take each chilled nipple and dip in the melted dark chocolate. Return to the parchment paper and leave to set for an hour.

Melt the white chocolate in a bain-marie. Take each dark-chocolate-covered nipple and dip the tip into the white chocolate. Leave to set. Enjoy!

Chocolate Pot

This is pure indulgence of the highest order. Try adding finely grated orange zest, or a dash of brandy, whisky or Kahlua, to make your own personal pot.

Preparation: 25 minutes
Chilling: overnight

Serves 6

250g dark chocolate (70 per cent cocoa)
750ml double cream
6 chocolate scrolls or 6 teaspoons crème fraiche, to serve

Break the chocolate into small pieces and put in a heatproof bowl. Place in a bain-marie (over a saucepan of simmering water) until almost melted. Heat the cream in a saucepan until just simmering, then add to the melted chocolate and blend until a smooth thick sauce has formed.

Pour into small ramekins or glasses, and leave to chill in the fridge overnight. Garnish with a chocolate scroll or a teaspoon of crème fraiche.

This is Lawrence's chocolate cake (see over): a cake so rich you can only serve it in slivers! Always line the tin with baking parchment (not greaseproof paper) to ensure you can easily release this rich, moist cake.

Gâteau Lawrence

This is a rich cake. If you find, as I do, that the chocolate icing seems a little too much of a good thing, try drizzling about 6 tablespoons of warmed apricot jam over the cake just before serving – the sharp tang of the fruit makes a wonderful contrast to the dark chocolate. Bliss!

Preparation: 30 minutes
Cooking: 50 minutes

Serves 6

For the cake:
180g dark chocolate (70 per cent cocoa)
175g butter, softened
125g unrefined sugar
200g ground almonds
4 eggs, separated

For the icing:
100g dark chocolate (70 per cent cocoa)
50g butter

Heat the oven to 150°C/gas 2.

Line a 25cm push-up-bottom or springform cake tin with baking parchment.

Break the chocolate into pieces and melt it in a bain-marie (that is, in a heatproof bowl over a pan of simmering water).

Cream together the butter and sugar until soft and creamy, using an electric whisk if you have one. Add the ground almonds, egg yolks and melted chocolate, and beat until evenly blended.

Whisk the egg whites until stiff, add to the cake mixture and quickly fold in until evenly mixed using a large metal spoon. Pour into the prepared cake tin and bake for 35 minutes. A light crust will form on the top and the middle should still be a little squishy. Leave to cool a little before carefully removing from the tin.

For the icing, melt the chocolate and butter in a bain-marie, drizzle over the cake and leave to set.

My brother Lawrence discovered this luscious chocolate cake, which uses ground almonds instead of flour for an incredibly moist and gooey consistency.

Anouchka's Chocolate Cake

My daughter usually prefers fresh mangoes to chocolate, but sometimes makes an exception in the case of this very special two-chocolate cake.

Preparation: 40 minutes
Cooking: 35 minutes

Serves 6

For the cake:
180g butter, softened
180g unrefined brown sugar
40g dark chocolate (70 per cent cocoa)
3 eggs
50g ground almonds
130g self-raising flour

For the icing:
190g unrefined icing sugar
25g butter, softened, cut into pieces
70ml hot milk
30g cocoa powder
20g white chocolate, grated
20g dark chocolate, grated

Heat the oven to 180°C/gas 4. Butter a 20cm push-up-bottom or springform cake tin.

   Cream together the butter and sugar with an electric whisk until creamy and fluffy. Melt the chocolate in a bain-marie (that is, in a heatproof bowl over a pan of simmering water). Break the eggs into the butter and sugar one at a time and whisk. The mixture will split, but don't worry – it will come back once you add the flour. Add the melted chocolate and ground almonds and blend well. Fold in the flour with a large metal spoon, then transfer the mixture to the cake tin.

   Bake for 35 minutes, or until the cake has come away from the sides of the tin, or a knife inserted into it comes out clean. Allow the cake to cool in the tin for 5 minutes before turning out. Then cool completely before icing it.

   To make the icing, sift the icing sugar into a bowl, add the butter pieces and mix with a fork. In a separate small bowl, pour the milk over the cocoa powder and mix until dissolved, then add this to the icing sugar and blend. Spread over the cake and then decorate with grated chocolate.

No Bake Crunch Cake

I used to make this absurdly simple cake over my single gas-ring when I was at university, and leave it to chill on my window-ledge overnight. It got me through a lot of late-night revision crises, and it's a great way to use up broken biscuits.

Preparation: 25 minutes
Chilling: 2 hours

Serves 6

150g butter
3 tbsp golden syrup
1 tbsp black treacle
200g dark chocolate (70 per cent cocoa)
150g mixed dried sultanas or raisins
75g glacé cherries
75g dried apricots
150g mixed nuts and seeds, chopped
1 x 250g packet digestive biscuits
unrefined icing sugar for dusting

Line a square 23cm low-sided baking tin with baking parchment.

   Carefully melt the butter, golden syrup, black treacle and chocolate in a saucepan over a low heat.

   Place the sultanas or raisins, glacé cherries, apricots, nuts and seeds in a bowl.

   Roughly crush the digestive biscuits (the best way is to place them in a strong plastic bag and break them up with a rolling pin) and add to the fruits in the bowl. Pour in the melted butter mix, stir, and transfer to the prepared tin. Smooth out and leave to set in the fridge for 2 hours.

   Dust with icing sugar and then cut into fingers with a sharp knife.

Roulade Bicolore

This two-tone cake combines two kinds of chocolate for a melting contrast of flavours. Topped with chocolate curls, it makes a spectacular Yule log or celebration cake.

Preparation: 30 minutes
Cooking: 45 minutes

Serves 6

For the roulade:
60g dark chocolate (70 per cent cocoa)
50g butter
150g unrefined light muscovado sugar
2 eggs
1 tbsp Kahlua liqueur
2 tbsp milk
150g self-raising flour

For the filling:
250ml double cream
125g white chocolate, grated
1/2 tsp vanilla extract

For the decoration:
30g white chocolate, grated
30g dark chocolate (70 per cent cocoa), grated

Heat the oven to 180°C/gas 4.

Line a 36cm x 25cm tin with baking parchment. First make the roulade. Break the chocolate into pieces and melt in a bain-marie (that is, in a heatproof bowl over a pan of simmering water).

Place the butter and sugar in a bowl and whisk until creamy and fluffy using an electric whisk. Add the eggs and continue to beat – the mixture will split but this is normal. Pour in the melted chocolate and mix well. Add the Kahlua and milk, and mix until smooth. Fold in the flour, then place the mixture in the prepared tin and spread it out evenly. Bake for 10 minutes. Remove from the oven, take the cake out of the tin and leave to cool on a wire rack until cold.

To make the filling, whisk the cream until it stands in very soft peaks using an electric whisk. Lightly mix in the grated chocolate and vanilla. Take care not to overwhip the cream or it will lose its light, soft texture. Place the cooled roulade on the work surface, baking-parchment side down, and spread the filling on top, keeping a space clear all around the edge.

Use the parchment paper to help you roll up the roulade into a log. Wrap the paper around the roulade and shape it with your hands into a smooth log, allow to sit for 5 minutes, then transfer on to a serving plate, removing the paper. Top with dark and white chocolate shavings.

A roulade is a marvellous thing, but difficult to serve.
A serrated knife is likely to break it up, so use a
sharp fine knife to cut it, and a palette knife to help to
hold it together.

Chocolate Cheesecake

It takes willpower to wait out the three-hour chilling time for this exceptional cheesecake – I find that I need an extra 200g of those chocolate-chip cookies to help me through it.

Preparation: 45minutes
Chilling: 3 hours

Serves 6

200g chocolate chip cookies, crushed
1/2 tsp cinnamon
100g butter, melted
100g dark chocolate (70 per cent cocoa)
1 tbsp Kahlua or Tia Maria liqueur
100g white chocolate
1 vanilla pod
225ml crème fraiche
75g unrefined demerara sugar
225ml double cream

Put the chocolate chip cookie crumbs in a bowl, add the cinnamon and melted butter, mix well and tip into a 22cm push-up-bottom or springform tin. Spread the mixture out evenly. Chill in the fridge until hard and set.

Melt the dark chocolate in a bain-marie (in a heatproof bowl over a pan of simmering water). Stir in the Kahlua or Tia Maria. Grate the white chocolate. Cut the vanilla pod in half lengthways, scrape out the seeds and add to the grated white chocolate.

Beat together the crème fraiche and demerara sugar until blended, then add the double cream and mix until smooth. Divide the mixture into 2 bowls. Add the melted dark chocolate and liqueur to the mixed creams in one bowl, and add the grated white chocolate and vanilla seeds to the other.

Spoon the two chocolate mixtures on to the chilled biscuit base and lightly mix with a fork to obtain a marbled effect. Chill for 3 hours before serving.

A truly special dessert: rich, dense and fragrant.
The marbled effect is easy to achieve, and for an
even more spectacular result, decorate with
chocolate curls or chocolate rose leaves.

Easy Chocolate Ice Cream

This grown-up chocolate ice cream, *Glâce 'Express' au Chocolat*, is from Janick Gestin of Laillé. Serve with your favourite toppings; chocolate curls, *crème Chantilly*, iced Kahlua or toasted almonds.

Preparation: 35 minutes
Freezing: 2 hours

Serves 6

150g dark or milk chocolate (70 per cent cocoa)
250ml milk
2 tbsp Kahlua liqueur
1 whole egg and 2 egg yolks
75g unrefined caster sugar
1 level tsp cornflour
350ml double cream

Break the chocolate into small pieces and place in a saucepan with the milk and Kahlua. Set over a low heat and stir until the chocolate has melted. Remove from the heat.

Place the egg and egg yolks with the sugar and cornflour in a heatproof bowl and beat until creamy and fluffy using an electric whisk. Pour in the melted chocolate and whisk well. Make a bain-marie and heat the mixture over a pan of simmering water, stirring constantly, until it begins to thicken (10–15 minutes). Remove from the heat and allow to cool a little.

Pour the cream into a bowl and whisk until it stands in soft peaks, then fold it into the chocolate mixture.

If you have an ice cream machine use it from here. If not, transfer the ice cream to a suitable container and leave in the freezer for 1 hour. Remove, beat the ice cream until smooth and return it to the freezer. Repeat until the ice cream has small crystals and can retain a good shape.

Chocolate Fondue

I love the informality of fondues and the picnic atmosphere they create. This sweet, light version is a perfect way to end a cheerful, noisy party. Use sweet almond oil if you can find it, but you can also make a good chocolate fondue without it.

Preparation: 25 minutes
Cooking: 15 minutes

Serves 6

For the fondue:
300g dark chocolate (70 per cent cocoa)
1 tbsp sweet almond oil, optional
100ml double cream
1 tbsp cognac

For dipping:
strawberries, apricot halves, pear slices, banana slices, peach slices, mandarin segments or small pieces of sponge cake

Break the chocolate into small pieces, put in a heatproof dish and melt in a bain-marie (over a pan of simmering water). Then add the oil, if using, the cream and cognac, and stir to make a glossy sauce for dipping. Transfer to a fondue bowl and keep warm with a night-light or burner. Serve the fondue at the table with dipping forks and all the dipping ingredients.

Chocolate Meringues

These luscious meringues are wonderful with *crème Chantilly* and fresh fruit.

Preparation: 15 minutes
Cooking: 2 hours

Serves 6

For the meringues:
3 egg whites
180g unrefined caster sugar
25g cocoa powder, sifted

For the *crème Chantilly*:
300ml whipping cream
25g unrefined caster sugar
1 tbsp Kahlua liqueur
chocolate (70 per cent cocoa) for decoration

Heat the oven to 140°C/gas 1.

Put the egg whites in a bowl and whisk rapidly until stiff, using an electric whisk if you have one. Add the caster sugar and whisk rapidly for another minute. Add the cocoa powder and whisk until blended.

Line a baking tray with baking parchment and scoop the meringue mixture on to the paper in 12 spoonfuls. Bake for 2 hours. For perfect crisp and dry meringues, turn the oven off but leave the meringues in there for another 12 hours.

Whisk the cream a little, add the sugar and Kahlua and continue to whisk carefully until it stands in soft peaks. Sandwich the meringues together with the Chantilly cream, and then, using a vegetable peeler, make chocolate curls and use them to decorate the meringues.

These beautiful meringues are a feature of many
elegant French *pâtisseries*, like fluffy caramel-
coloured clouds above the multicoloured fruit
tarts and sculptural *pièces montées*.

Long before chocolate came to us from South America, the Aztecs drank an infusion of cacao spiced with pepper and chilli as part of their religious ceremonies. Later, as drinking chocolate gained popularity in Europe, sugar and milk were added to sweeten the bitter taste, and the strong spices were no longer needed to make it palatable.

Vianne's Spiced Hot Chocolate

Chilli may have lost favour as an ingredient in chocolate dishes in Europe, but for me this sweet, spiced version of hot chocolate is the best morning drink: rich, dark and invigorating enough to keep me going until lunchtime.

Preparation: 10 minutes
Cooking: 15 minutes

Serves 2

400ml full-fat milk
1/2 vanilla pod, cut in half lengthways
1/2 cinnamon stick
1 hot chilli, halved and deseeded
100g dark chocolate (70 per cent cocoa)
unrefined brown sugar to taste
whipped cream, chocolate curls, cognac or
Amaretto to serve

Place the milk in a saucepan, add the vanilla pod, cinnamon stick and seedless chilli and gently bring it to a shivering simmer for 1 minute. Grate the chocolate and whisk it in until it melts. If you must, then add sugar, but do try it without. Take off the heat and allow it to infuse for 10 minutes, then remove the spices, return to the heat and bring gently back to simmering point. Serve in mugs topped with whipped cream, chocolate curls or a dash of cognac or Amaretto.

Index

Index of Recipe Titles

Conversion tables

Weights		Liquids		Oven temperatures		
5g	$1/4$ oz	15 ml	$1/2$ fl oz	110°C	225°F	gas mark $1/4$
15g	$1/2$ oz	25ml	1 fl oz	120°C	250°F	gas mark $1/2$
20g	$3/4$ oz	50ml	2 fl oz	140°C	275°F	gas mark 1
25g	1oz	75ml	3 fl oz	150°C	300°F	gas mark 2
50g	2oz	100ml	$31/2$ fl oz	160°C	325°F	gas mark 3
75g	3oz	125ml	4 fl oz	180°C	350°F	gas mark 4
125g	4oz	150ml	$1/4$ pint	190°C	375°F	gas mark 5
150g	5oz	175ml	6 fl oz	200°C	400°F	gas mark 6
175g	6oz	200ml	7 fl oz	220°C	425°F	gas mark 7
200g	7oz	250ml	8 fl oz	230°C	450°F	gas mark 8
250g	8oz	275ml	9 fl oz	240°C	475°F	gas mark 9
275g	9oz	300ml	$1/2$ pint			
300g	10oz	325ml	11 fl oz			
325g	11oz	350ml	12 fl oz			
375g	12oz	375ml	13 fl oz			
400g	13oz	400ml	14 fl oz			
425g	14oz	450ml	$3/4$ pint			
475g	15oz	475ml	16 fl oz			
500g	1lb	500ml	17 fl oz			
625g	$11/4$lb	550ml	18 fl oz			
750g	$11/2$lb	600ml	1 pint			
875g	$13/4$lb	750ml	$11/4$ pints			
1kg	2 lb	900ml	$11/2$ pints			
1.25kg	$21/2$lb	1 litre	$13/4$ pints			
1.5kg	3lb	1.2 litres	2 pints			
1.75kg	$31/2$lb	1.5 litres	$21/2$ pints			
2kg	4 lb	1.8 litres	3 pints			

Acknowledgements

The French kitchen is a sociable place where anybody can help out, whether they are doing the cooking, preparing the vegetables or simply telling stories to help the others pass the time. Heartfelt thanks to the many, many people who contributed ideas, recipes, photographs and all the other ingredients which make up this book; especially photographer Debi Treloar, designer Kenneth Carroll, jacket illustrator Stuart Haygarth and jacket designer Claire Ward, art director Liz Laczynska, editors Alison Tulett, Mari Roberts and Francesca Liversidge, and Warrior Maidens Serafina Clarke and Jennifer Luithlen. Thanks also to everyone who contributed ideas and recipes, including all the members of the Payen and Sorin families, Joanne's mother Jeannette Payen Short, Joanne's brother Lawrence, Jean and Simone Sorin, Claudine Pénisson, Denise Douazan and Mikaël Quaireau. Many thanks, too, to Marité and André Roty, Monique and Hamadi Kachkachi, Josette and Jacques Crochet, Juliette and Joseph Jeuland, Pierre and Janick Gestin, and Danielle and Michel Stéphan for all their help and their generous hospitality to our team during their stay in France.

We would like to thank Vicki Keppel-Compton and Laura Lenox Conyngham for recipe testing, and Vicki for assisting on the recipe shoot; Helen Trent for styling; and the following generous suppliers and hospitable hosts in both England and France.

The French House
78 York Street
London W1H 1DP
020 7298 6189
www.thefrench-house.com

M & C Vegetables
Turnham Green Terrace
London W4 1RG
020 8995 0140
www.m-and-c.co.uk

Mortimer and Bennet Deli
Turnham Green Terrace
London W4 1RG
020 8995 4145

Covent Garden Fishmongers
Turnham Green Terrace
London W4 1RG
020 8995 9273

Macken Brothers Butchers
Turnham Green Terrace
London W4 1RG
020 8994 2646

Farmers' markets everywhere:
see www.farmersmarkets.net

Chalmers & Grey Fishmongers
67 Notting Hill Gate
London W11 3JS
020 7221 6177

Paul Bakery
115 Marylebone High Street
London W1U 4SB
020 7836 3304

Eurostar (UK) Limited
Waterloo Station
London SE1 8SE
08705 186 186
eurostar.com

Brittany Ferries
0870 5 360 360
www.brittanyferries.com

Aux Crus de Bourgogne
3 rue Bachaumont
75002 Paris
01 42 33 48 24

La Fromagerie 31
64 rue de Seine
75006 Paris
01 43 26 50 31

E. Dehillerin
18 et 20 rue Coquillière
75001 Paris
01 42 36 53 13

Hotel Aviatic
105 rue de Vaugirard
75006 Paris
01 53 63 25 50

Da Rosa
Epicurie Fine
62 rue de Seine
75006 Paris
01 40 51 00 09

Gerrard Judd
La Castafiore
51 rue St Louis en L'Île
75004 Paris

Segolene & Charles de Valbray
Château de Saint Patern
72610 Saint Patern
02 33 27 54 71
www.chateau-saintpaterne.com

Marquis et Marquise Gicquel
des Touches
Château de Sarceaux
61250 Valframbert
02 33 28 85 11
www.chateauxcountry.com
/chateaux/sarceaux

Joanne Harris and Fran Warde

Special Dedication

Given that my role in all this has been one of maximum enjoyment and minimum effort, I am donating my share of the proceeds to the humanitarian organization Médecins Sans Frontières, who are unique among aid charities in that they are entirely secular, non-judgemental and one hundred percent committed to helping the sick and the afflicted wherever they are and regardless of race, religion, or political affiliation. This book is dedicated to them, and to everyone who has not yet discovered the pleasures of their own kitchen - what are you waiting for?

Joanne Harris

Médecins Sans Frontières

Providing emergency medical relief to populations in danger

When an epidemic rages out of control, when a rain of shells reduces a town to ruins, when an area of conflict is too dangerous for most aid agencies to enter, MSF's skilled medical teams are there.

Médecins Sans Frontières (MSF) is the leading non-governmental organization for emergency medical aid. We provide independent medical relief to victims of war, disasters and epidemics in over eighty countries around the world, treating those who need it most, regardless of ethnic origin, religion or political affiliation.

Initially founded in Paris in 1971, MSF has become an international organization with support offices in 20 countries. Every year MSF sends around 2,500 volunteer doctors, nurses and technical support staff to some of the most far flung regions of the world to care for those most in need.

To get access to, and care for, those most vulnerable, MSF must remain scrupulously independent of governments as well as of religious and economic powers. We rely on private individuals for the majority of our funding.

You can contact us at:
Médecins Sans Frontières (UK)
67-74 Saffron Hill
London EC1N 8QX

Tel: 020 7404 6600
Fax: 020 7404 4466
e-mail: office-ldn@london.msf.org
website: www.uk.msf.org

oeufs

sel

pa

Prepar

Propork